D1218792

VOL 5: THE ONE

"Amazing! It hit all the right notes, and got the Doctor perfect! 9/10"
COMIC BOOK CAST

"A truly fantastic Doctor Who adventure that rewards loyal readers and long-time fans of the show."
POP CULTURE BANDIT

"Great characterization and a sense of adventure! 9/10"
COMICS VERSE

"Fun, energetic events liven things up with some thrilling twists!"
SNAPPOW

"An enjoyable romp."
FLICKERING MYTH

"9.5 out of 10!"
NERDS UNCHAINED

"Does a splendid job of capturing Matt Smith's expressions."
GEEK WITH CURVES

"The tone of the Eleventh Doctor is strong in this one."
WARPED FACTOR

"A fantastic Eleventh Doctor adventure! 9 out of 10!"
NEWSARAMA

"A great job creating a companion who can keep up with the Doctor. 10 out of 10!"
PROJECT FANDOM

"Nails the tone and spirit right out of the gate. 4 out of 5!"
COMIC BOOK RESOURCES

"A great continuation of a fabulous series. The character depth, dramatic arc, and suspenseful flow make it a gripping read."
UNLEASH THE FANBOY

"Excellent script with great artwork. I've become a fan of Alice Obiefune – what a character she has become!"
TM STASH

"Compelling art."
BLEEDING COOL

"Leaves you wanting more!"
BLOGTOR WHO

TITAN COMICS

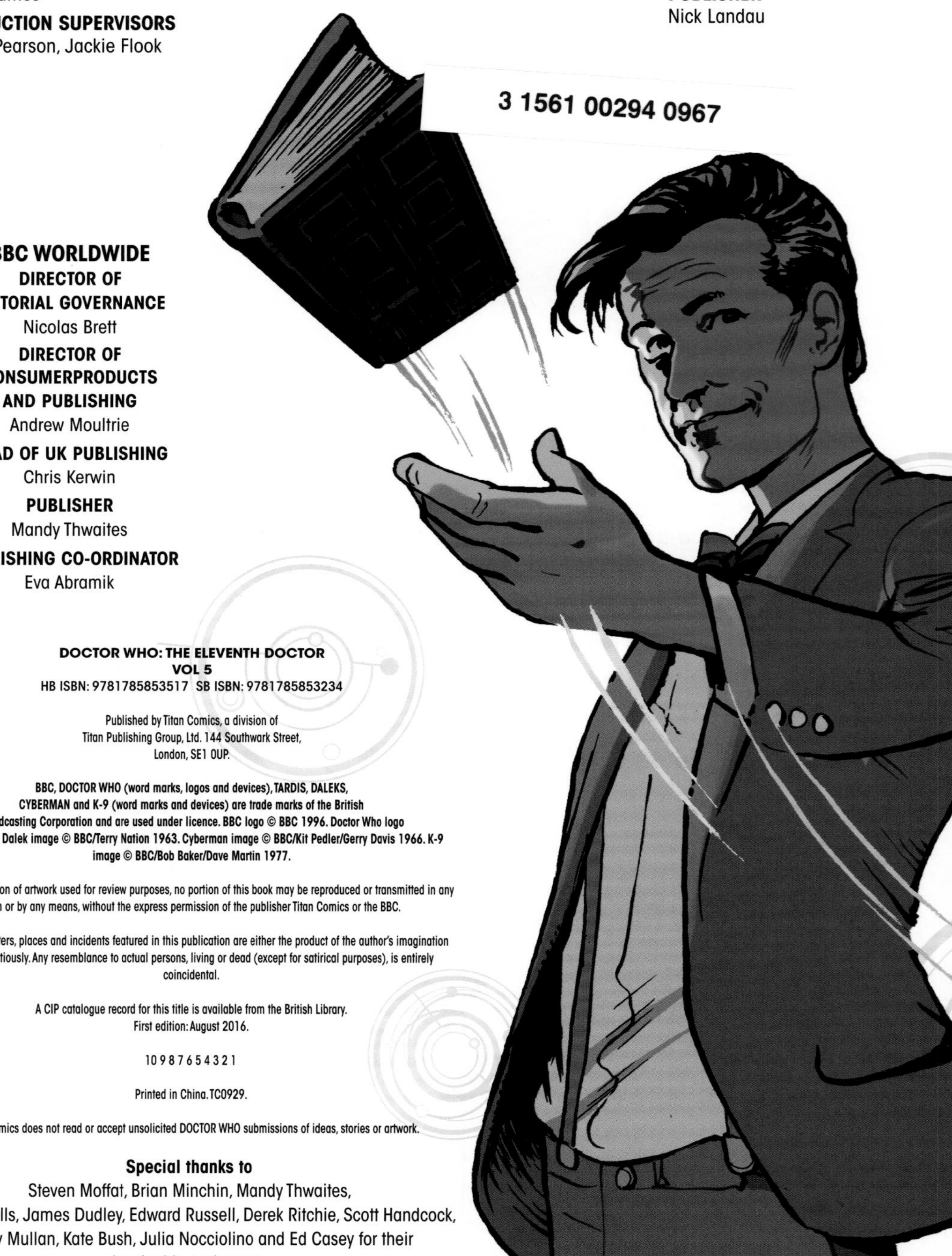

DOCTOR WHO: THE ELEVENTH DOCTOR
VOL 5
HB ISBN: 9781785853517 SB ISBN: 9781785853234

Published by Titan Comics, a division of
Titan Publishing Group, Ltd. 144 Southwark Street,
London, SE1 0UP.

A CIP catalogue record for this title is available from the British Library.
First edition: August 2016.

10 9 8 7 6 5 4 3 2 1

Printed in China. TC0929.

Special thanks to
Steven Moffat, Brian Minchin, Mandy Thwaites, Matt Nicholls, James Dudley, Edward Russell, Derek Ritchie, Scott Handcock, Kirsty Mullan, Kate Bush, Julia Nocciolino and Ed Casey for their invaluable assistance.

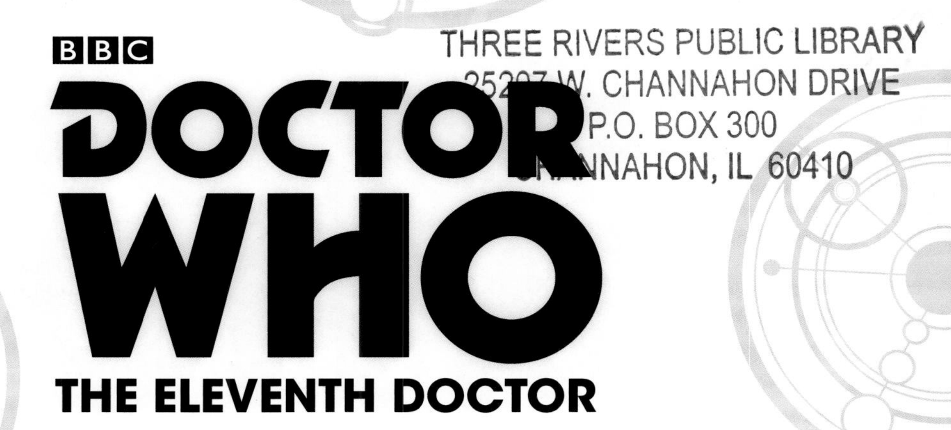

THE ELEVENTH DOCTOR

VOL 5: THE ONE

WRITERS:
SI SPURRIER & ROB WILLIAMS

ARTISTS:
SIMON FRASER
WARREN PLEECE
LEANDRO CASCO
LEONARDO ROMERO
INK ASSISTS ON CHAPTER 8 BY ADRIANO VICENTE, WELLINGTON DIAS & RAPHAEL LOBOSCO

COLORISTS:
GARY CALDWELL, HI-FI
ROD FERNANDES, ARIANNA FLOREAN,
NICOLA RIGHI WITH AZZURRA FLOREAN

LETTERS: RICHARD STARKINGS AND COMICRAFT'S JIMMY BETANCOURT

ABSLOM DAAK CREATED BY STEVE MOORE AND STEVE DILLON

ABSLOM DAAK APPEARS COURTESY OF **PANINI COMICS**
WITH THANKS TO THE AMAZING TEAM AT **DOCTOR WHO MAGAZINE**.
VISIT ***DOCTORWHOMAGAZINE.COM*** TO SUBSCRIBE AND FIND OUT MORE.

BBC

www.titan-comics.com

ALICE OBIEFUNE

Former Library Assistant Alice Obiefune felt like her life was falling apart – then she met the Doctor! Now she's determined to see all the beauty and strangeness of the universe as she travels with him in the TARDIS!

THE DOCTOR

The last of the Time Lords of Gallifrey, the Eleventh Doctor is an old soul in the body of a boy professor. Though he makes mistakes – and often! – he *never* runs away from the consequences. Apart from days like today, when running seems like the best idea!

THE TARDIS

'Time and Relative Dimension in Space'. Bigger on the inside this unassuming blue box is yo ticket to unforgettable adventur The Doctor likes to think he's in control, but often the TARDIS takes him where and when he needs to be...

PREVIOUSLY...

The Overcast blamed the Doctor for the death of their people, and hired The Then and The Now, a temporal bounty hunter, to punish him. Unable to shake this impossible tail, the Doctor, Alice and their unlikely passengers ventured to worlds devastated by the Time War to try and prove his innocence. But when a lone white pillar keeps cropping up, this time as the emblem of a renegade faction of Sontarans at war with their own kind, The Doctor believes he knows who framed him... someone *Master*ful! As such, he's going to need the help of a dear old friend: Professor River Song! He just has to break her out of prison first...

When you've finished reading the collection, please email your thoughts to doctorwhocomic@titanemail.com

OBSESSIONS

YOU'RE FEELING SORRY FOR YOURSELF, DOCTOR. I CAN TELL.
OKAY, I'VE GOT A QUESTION FOR YOU...
WHY DO YOU DO WHAT YOU DO?

...WHAT?
BECAUSE, ALICE OBIEFUNE, I AM THE DOCT...
NO, NOT THAT. I DIDN'T ASK FOR A BIG SPEECH OR STIRRING MUSIC. I KNOW YOU'RE THE DOCTOR.
WHAT I WANT TO KNOW IS WHY YOU KEEP TRAVELING THROUGH TIME AND SPACE WITH AN ENTOURAGE. YOU'RE ALWAYS BUMPING INTO TROUBLE AND MONSTERS TRYING TO KILL PEOPLE AND ALL THAT. IT'S HARD WORK. WHY D--
WHIRRRRRRRRRRRRRRRR
TALKING! TALKING TALKING TALKING!
LESS TALKING! MORE CUTTING! MORE RENDING AND THE HITTING!
I GENUINELY DON'T KNOW HOW MUCH LONGER I CAN STAND YOU PEOPLE. ALL YOU DO IS BLAH! BLAH! BLAH!
TARDIS TOOK MY WIFE. I'M OFF TO FIND HER. OR MAYBE I'LL START SLICIN' THROUGH TARDIS WALLS! THROUGH TARDIS OWNERS!

RAAAAAAAAAA!
CASE IN POINT: ABSLOM DAAK. HOMICIDAL MANIAC WITH A CHAINSWORD. WHY ON EARTH WOULD YOU MAKE IT YOUR JOB TO FERRY HIM ROUND?
IT'S NOT ME, ALICE. THE TARDIS HID HIS WIFE'S BODY.

I'M NOT THE ONE KEEPING HIM HERE...
HMMM. I KNOW THAT LOOK. WHAT YOU UP TO?
WELL... IF YOU REALLY MUST KNOW...

"...THE RANTING LOON RATHER REMINDS ME OF SOMEONE.
"SOMEONE VERY DEAR TO ME.

"MYSELF, ACTUALLY.
...TAKE MY WIFE, WILL THEY...

IDIOTS. DID THEY THINK I'D NOT HAVE A TRACE ON SOMETHIN AS PRECIOU AS MY WIFE.
DEAD WIFE.

"A HOMICIDAL KILLER WHO CHOSE EXILE TO A DALEK WORLD AS HIS PUNISHMENT. THE ACCEPTED WISDOM BEING THAT HE'D BE DEAD IN MINUTES.
I MADE THE DALEKS FEAR ME!
THE DALEKS! SCARED OF NOTHIN' AND THEY RAN FROM ME! I SHOWED 'EM WHAT EXTERMINATION REALLY MEANT.
"IT DIDN'T QUITE WORK OUT THAT WAY, OF COURSE...
"WE ALL HAVE TO FIND OUR JOY, ALICE.
"DAAK'S WAS KILLING LOTS AND LOTS OF DALEKS.
THEY REMEMBER ME!
THEY REMEMBER US!

YOU'VE LOST ME. YOU'RE NOT REMOTELY LIKE THAT.
NOT IN SOME WAYS, NO. BUT...
WELL, IT'S ALL ABOUT GOALS ALICE OBIEFUNE.
"YOU REACH A POINT WHEN YOU'VE SEEN SO MUCH OF THE GALAXY...
"ENCOUNTERED SO MUCH HORROR...
...STUPID TARDIS...
"THAT UNLESS YOU HAVE A... SINGULARITY OF PURPOSE, YOU WILL SIMPLY GO FLAPPING OFF INTO CHAOS AND INSANITY.
"IT'S ALL... TOO BIG, YOU SEE.
"IT'S TOO MUCH.
"I THINK WE ALL RATHER CHOOSE OUR OBSESSIONS...

"--AND MAKE THEM INTO BODYGUARDS TO PROTECT US.
--RRRRRR SMASH EVERY STUPID BLUE BOX I EVER SEE W--

"Y'SEE, ALICE... DAAK'S WIFE... IN A CERTAIN LIGHT, FOR A PARTICULAR SORT OF PERSON, SHE'S THE PERFECT PARTNER.
T...TAIYIN?
"THINK ABOUT IT. SHE'LL NEVER BETRAY HIM, NEVER HATE HIM, NEVER FALL SHORT OF HIS EXPECTATIONS.
"SHE'S A NEATLY-PACKAGED, ETERNALLY LOYAL MEANS TO AN END.

LIKE A TARDIS, YOU MEAN?
HA. WELL... PERHAPS ON A SUPERFICAL SORT OF LEVEL.
LOOK, THE POINT IS, YOU CAN SEE WHY HE'S SO FIXATED ON GETTING HER BACK.

YOU 'N ME, TAI. WE CAN FINALLY GET OUTTA HERE! GET BACK TO THE GOOD OLD WAYS!
BLAZIN' ACROSS THE GALAXY! FIGHTIN' AND DRINKIN' AND... AND...
YEAH. THAT'S THE LIFE. NO MORE TIME-SNOBS AN' GOODIE-TWO-SHOES COMPANIONS.

JUST, Y'KNOW. CRUISIN'. TRYINNA RAISE SOME CASH.
LOOKIN' FER... DALEKS TO KILL. AND SO FORTH.
JUST, AH.
JUST THE TWO OF US.

DOCTOR... YOU OKAY?
MMM?
OH... YES, OF COURSE. IT'S JUST... WELL, THIS IS RATHER THE POINT, ALICE:

"OBSESSIONS ARE ALL VERY WELL TO KEEP ONE GOING-- BUT THEY'RE ALSO RATHER NIFTY AT BRINGING YOU TO A SKIDDING HALT.

IF YOU'RE GOING TO BE REALLY CLEVER ABOUT... NOT BEING EATEN BY THE VOID... NOT BEING SQUASHED BY THE SHEER GARGANTUAN CHAOS OF IT ALL...
...ALL THAT JAZZ...
...THEN YOU REALLY ONLY HAVE TWO CHOICES.
KIK

NE: YOU ACCEPT THAT E THINGS WHICH KEEP OU GOING ARE ONLY ER TEMPORARY, AND U PREPARE TO SWITCH OBSESSIONS LIKE CLOTHING.
"OR TWO: YOU MAKE YOUR MISSION SO IMPOSSIBLE YOU'LL NEVER EVER SUCCEED.

BUT THEN--
MM?
HEY, WAIT... YOUR BUM'S GLOWING...
AH, WHOOPS. SITTING ON THE INTERCOM SWITCH AGAIN.

WHAT A SILLY OLD THING I AM.

SO... OKAY... WHICH STRATEGY DO YOU TAKE, OH CRYPTIC SENSEI? THE EVER-CHANGING GOAL OR THE ENDLESS MISSION?
...HA. COME NOW, MY DEAR LIBRARIAN.
A DOCTOR TREATS ONE PATIENT AT A TIME...IN THE CERTAIN KNOWLEDGE THERE ARE ALWAYS MORE.
BOTH, ALICE OBIEFUNE.
I LIVE BY BOTH.
HEY!

ARE YOU STILL TALKING? IS THAT ALL YOU DO?!
I SWEAR, THE SECOND I FIND MY WIFE I'M GONNA SLICE THIS DAMN BOX TA BLUE RIBBONS AN' SHOW YA HOW FAR TALKIN' REALLY GETS YA.

YOU DIDN'T FIND HER YET, THEN?
AIN'T THAT OBVIOUS?! YA THINK I'D STILL BE AROUND IF I DID?!
BUT I WILL, DAMN YOU! AND I'M STAYIN' RIGHT HERE 'TIL I DO!

NOW WHERE THE HELL DID I PUT THAT WHISKY?
SERIOUSLY, DOCTOR... I THINK YOU'RE WAY OFF WITH THIS ONE.
HE'S NOTHING LIKE YOU.

VZK

POLICE

POLICE PUBLIC CALL

RIVER SONG.
"TIME TRAVELER. CRIMINAL. MURDERER... MAYBE... ARCHAEOLOGIST... APPARENTLY... EVENTUALLY. AND I HATE ARCHAEOLOGISTS...
"I GIVE HER MY SONIC... ONE DAY.
"I TELL HER MY NAME.
"...
"...MY REAL NAME.
HE KNOWS THINGS I'M NG TO DO THAT I DON'T. D THAT, WHEN YOU'RE A E TRAVELER WITH AN IQ AS BIG AS EINSTEIN'S QUANTUM PANTS...
"THAT IS VERY, EXTREMELY ANNOYING.
"AND THAT SMILE. LOOK AT HER. SO COCKY. THINKS SHE CAN READ ME. ME? UNREADABLE ME. THINKS SHE KNOWS WHAT I'M GOING TO SAY BEFORE I EVEN..."
WHY ME?

...
WELL THAT'S ANNOYING.

LOOK, JUST TO BE CLEAR, I ABSOLUTELY WAS NOT THINKING THAT THE SECOND BEFORE YOU SAID IT. COMPRENDE?
ABSOLUTELY, SWEETIE.
WE'VE TALKED ABOUT THIS! THE NORMAL DYNAMIC IS I SAY IMPRESSIVE, CLEVER THINGS AND PEOPLE LOOK VERY SURPRISED AT THE IMPRESSIVE, CLEVER STUFF I'VE COME UP WITH.

THE SMARTEST PERSON IN THE ROOM... YOU DO LIKE BELIEVING YOU KNOW WHAT OTHERS ARE THINKING BEFORE THEY DO...
IT GETS VERY LONELY IN THIS CELL, YOU KNOW.
DO YOU KNOW WHAT I'M THINKING NOW?

ARE YOU... BLUSHING?
HRM... SHE HAS THE ARDOR.
DOCTOR? ARE YOU UNWELL? YOU APPEAR BILLIOUS.

AHHHHH, SO YOU'RE ALICE. DON'T BELIEVE WE'VE HAD THE PLEASURE. THE SIDE COMPANION.
DON'T TAKE THIS WRONG AND ALL, BUT WHO THE HELL ARE YOU?
SHE'S FEISTY...! FOR A LIBRARY ASSISTANT.

SHE GOT THAT RIGHT... FIRST TIME.
ARGH. SHE KNOWS THINGS. SOME THINGS. SHE KNOWS THE FUTURE ME. OBVIOUSLY SHE'S MET YOU. OR I'VE TOLD HER ABOUT YOU. OR...
PLEASE DON'T MENTION LIBRARIES, RIVER. IT MAKES MY HEAD HURT.

YOU HAVEN'T ANSWERED MY QUESTION.
WHY ME?

I NEED TO BREAK INTO SOMEWHERE IMPOSSIBLE AND STEAL SOMETHING. AND I NEED A DEVIOUS CRIMINAL MIND FOR THAT.
SO I THOUGHT OF YOU.

THAT'S VERY NICE AND SOUNDS WONDERFULLY EXCITING. AND IT'S TIME NOT SPENT IN THIS CELL AND IT'S A DATE, SO OF COURSE I'M IN. BUT...
WELL... IT'S NOT THE TRUTH, IS IT?

WHIRRR

NO, IT'S NOT.

WOOOEEEWOOOEEE

WHAT'S *THAT?*
TIMESTREAM ALARM. I PROGRAMMED THE TARDIS TO DETECT WHEN THE THEN AND THE NOW IS ABOUT TO MATERIALIZE. IT'S RIGHT BEHIND US.
WOOOEEEWOOOEEE

I'M SURE, WHATEVER THAT IS... IT'S *TERRIFYING.*
GO ON, DO IT. FOR ME.

YOU KNOW YOU WANT TO.

OH, ALRIGHT...
CLICK
THE ONE
PART 1
WOOOEEEWOOOEEE
GO ON THEN.

VWOORRRP VWOORRRP
STILL LEAVE THE BRAKES ON, I SEE.

OKAY. YOU WANT TO KNOW WHY YOU?
WHY NOW?
POLICE BOX

YOUR DIARY, RIVER. NO MORE TEASES. NO MORE CUTESY LTTLE REFERENCES TO "SPOILERS".
THIS IS SERIOUS. I'VE BEEN ACCUSED OF SOMETHING. AND I... WELL...
THIS IS SERIOUS.

I WON'T TELL YOU YOUR FUTURE.
NO. BUT YOU CAN TELL ME MY PAST.

THIS LOVELY, VIOLENT SEPTUAGENARIAN IN BATTLE ARMOR -- THE SQUIRE...
WELL MET!
...TELLS ME THAT SHE WAS MY COMPANION BACK IN THE TIME WAR. BUT I CAN'T REMEMBER HER.
AT ALL.
AND I CAN'T REMEMBER COMMITTING GENOCIDE EITHER. BUT THAT'S WHAT I'M CURRENTLY ACCUSED OF. AND IT CONNECTS, RIVER.

YOU'RE GENUINELY SPOOKED, AREN'T YOU?
ALRIGHT.

GO ON THEN. LOOK. GIVE IN!
YOU KNOW I CAN'T.
DOCTOR I HAVE READ THIS BOOK, COVER TO COVER. *MANY* TIMES. AND HERE'S WHAT I KNOW FOR A FACT.

POLICE PUBLIC CALL BOX
WHATEVER THIS CRIME YOU ARE SUPPOSED TO HAVE COMMITTED IS, YOU DID *NOT* COMMIT IT.
YOU'VE ALLOWED YOURSELF TO BE WEAKENED BY DOUBT WHEN YOUR USUAL LANGUAGE IS *CERTAINTY*....
SO, IF YOU DO NEED TO SEE HOW THE PATH AHEAD IS MAPPED OUT...

THE REAL REASON YOU CAME TO ME?
YOU NEEDED TO SEE SOMEONE WHO KNOWS YOU WHO WILL LOOK YOU IN THE EYE AND TELL YOU THAT YOU'RE GOOD.

READ IT IF YOU HAVE TO.
BUT I'LL MISS THE SMARTEST MAN IN THE ROOM UNRAVELLING HIS MYSTERIES.

I DON'T THINK YOU EVER WERE HIS COMPANION.
I'M VERY SORRY.

OH.

YOU CAN TAKE ME BACK TO STORMCAGE...

...NOW YOU'VE GOT ALL THE ANSWERS.

RIVER?

THINK I'LL WAIT FOR THE POP-UP BOOK VERSION.
CATCH.
FANCY HELPING ME BREAK INTO T MOST DANGER PRISON IN THIS ANY OTHER UNIVERSE?
I'VE GOT A REALLY BIG PLAN.

HELLO YOU.

BOOT

COUGH
THE *DUST.* WHEN WAS THE LAST TIME YOU CLEANED IN HERE?
DO YOU KNOW HOW MANY ROOMS ARE IN THE TARDIS? CAN'T BE EXPECTED TO CLEAN ALL OF THEM, CAN I?
TURN THE LIGHT ON!
K9

WHAT IS THIS PLACE?
OLD OFFICE. ALWAYS MEANT TO TIDY IT UP, BUT WHO HAS TIME FOR ALL THAT, EH?
AN IMMORTAL TIME LORD?
K9

TELL ME U DON'T LIKE THIS LOOK, SWEETIE.
WHY DOES SHE CALL YOU SWEETIE?
TO ANNOY ME. SHE KNOWS HOW LAZY I FIND CATCHPHRAS... *OOH.*

JELLY BABY?
U.N.I.T

WHAT'S THE "BEST BEFORE" DATE ON THESE?
DUNNO. LATE 70S? SHOULD BE FINE.
SO? WHERE'S YOUR BRILLIANT PLAN?

HERE.
Doctor! Don't go here! Because you left it here and it gets you there! Got it? GOOD!

CREAK
I LOVE A GOOD MAP, ME.

AH, IT IS STILL THERE. CLEVER ME.
POLICE BOX

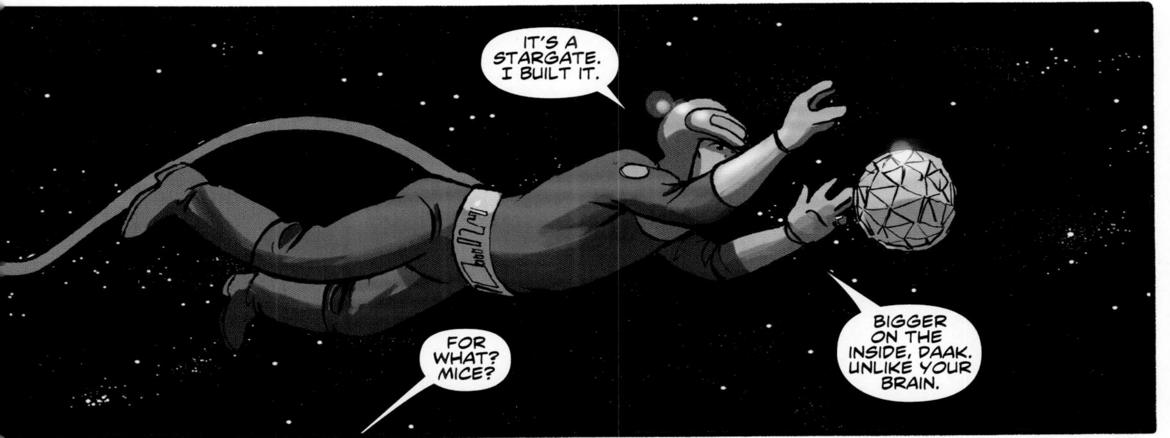
IT'S A STARGATE. I BUILT IT.
FOR WHAT? MICE?
BIGGER ON THE INSIDE, DAAK. UNLIKE YOUR BRAIN.

WHERE DOES IT LEAD, DOCTOR?
AND JUST *HOW* DANGEROUS ARE WE TALKING HERE?

THERE IS A PLACE WHERE *NO ONE* IS SUPPOSED TO GO. EVER. THE TIME LORDS SAW TO THAT.
NO ONE'S EVEN SUPPOSED TO *REMEMBER* THIS PLACE.
BUT I'VE *BEEN* THERE.

WANTED TO MAKE SURE I WAS NEVER TEMPTED TO GO BACK THERE. OR NO ONE COULD EVER GET ITS LOCATION FROM ME.
AND SO I MADE MYSELF FORGET THE PLACE'S *NAME*. LIKE WIPING OLD TV TAPES. I DELETED A COUPLE OF MY OWN BRAIN CELLS. IT'S FINE. I'VE GOT LOTS.
...BUT I BUILT *THIS* INSTEAD. TO ONLY ACTIVATE WITH MY DNA SIGNATURE. JUST IN CASE, Y'KNOW.

WOOOEEEWOOOEEE
DOCTOR! THE ALARM! WE'VE BEEN HERE TOO LONG.
THE THEN AND THE NOW IS *COMING!* WE HAVE TO *GO!*

NOT YET.
WOOOEEEWOOOEEE

WOOOEEE WOOOEEE
SPACE VIOLENCE IMMINENT. GOOD!
POLICE BOX
DOCTOR! WE CAN'T FIGHT IT! IT'LL KILL US ALL!

WOOOEEEWOOOEEE
HERE HE COMES.
WHO'S A PRETTY BOY THEN?
GET READY, RIVER!
WAIT UNTIL IT'S ATTACHED ITSELF TO THE TARDIS!

YOU WANT ME TO FLY THE TARDIS, DON'T YOU? YOU'RE NOT BRINGING THAT THING IN?
WE'RE THE BAIT!
YOU HAVEN'T EVEN TOLD ME WHAT WE'RE TRYING TO STEAL, YOU LUNATIC!
WOOOEEE WOOOEEE

I'D HAVE THOUGHT THAT WAS OBVIOUS...
THE MASTER'S TARDIS.

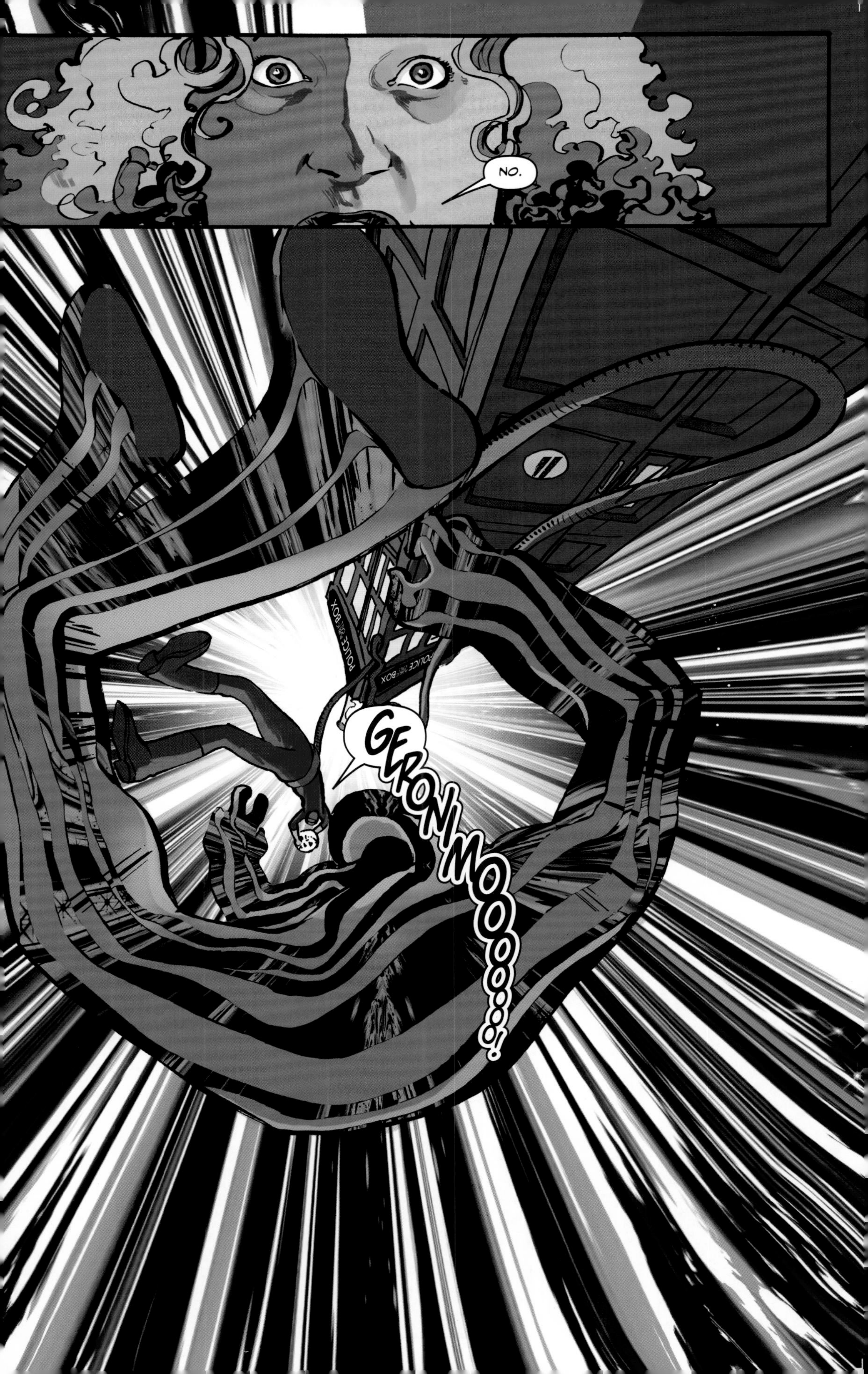
NO.
GERONIMOOOOOOO!

SHE'S GOING TOO FAST! THROUGH TOO MANY ERAS AT ONCE!
YOU CAN FLY THE TARDIS? I THOUGHT ONLY HE COULD FLY THE TARDIS?

THIS ISN'T FLYING, ALICE...
MORE... CONTROLLED FALLING!

THE THEN AND THE NOW IS WITH US!
IT CAME THROUGH TOO, DOCTOR! YOU WAITED TOO LONG!

HE INTENDED TO DO THAT.
THE DOCTOR ALWAYS HAS A PLAN!
SHE DOES KNOW YOU.
UH, RIVER. HATE TO BE A WORRY-WORT BUT WE ARE ABOUT TO HIT THE CHRONAL EQUIVALENT OF A BIG BRICK WALL. UNLESS YOU DO SOMETHING. QUICK.
WHAT?

IT'S ON THE ROOF!
THOOOM
IT'S COMING THROUGH!
RIVERRRRRRRR!
YOU KNOW THOSE BRAKES YOU'RE ALWAYS NAGGING ME ABOUT?
YES?
USE THEM!
NOW!

SKREEEEEEEEEEEEEEEEEEEEEEE
"HOW DO YOU BREAK INTO AN IMPOSSIBLE PRISON THAT IS CONTAINED WITHIN AN IMPOSSIBLE QUANTUM WALL?
POLICE BOX
"THROW SOMETHING IMPOSSIBLE AT IT.
"RIVER WAS VERY SWEET AND WE CAN ALL USE A LITTLE EMOTIONAL BOLSTERING EVERY NOW AND AGAIN...
KRAKKSSCCHHHHOOOOOOMM

POLICE PUBLIC CALL BOX
"... BUT I ALREADY KNOW THAT I AM VERY, VERY GOOD."
NOW, RIVER! WE'RE THROUGH! TAKE US THROUGH BEFORE THE WALLS REFORM!
LAND THE TARDIS!

WOORRRP
WOORRRP
LAND?

LAND WHERE?
IT'S HERE! WHATEVER THAT WAS, IT DIDN'T FINISH IT!

GOOD! SOME LEFT FOR DAAK!
VIOLENCE TIME!

WAIT. I KNOW I'M BEING A SPOILSPORT HERE BUT...
...TRUST YOUR DOCTOR, EH?

INTRUDER IDENTIFIED! INTRUDER IDENTIFIED!
SECURITY'S ABOUT TO TAKE ON OUR SOMEWHAT IRRITATING, IMMENSELY POWERFUL PURSUER FOR US.
HERE THEY COME...

TRUDER IDENTIFIED!
CHRONAL VIOLATION!
OBLITERATE AND PROTECT!
OBLITERATE AND PROTECT!
FSSSSHHHHZZZ
"AND THEN THE THEN AND THE NOW IS GOING TO TAKE CARE OF SECURITY FOR US.
OBLITERATE AND PROTE...
"HANDY, EH? IT'S ALMOST LIKE SOMEONE DASHING AND LUDICROUSLY CLEVER PLANNED IT."
...BY GOD DALEK BONES...
AHHHHH. THAT'S WHAT IT'S CALLED! I'D FORGOTTEN THE NAME BUT NOW...IT'S ALL COME BACK TO ME. OF COURSE! FIVE LITTLE LETTERS.
DOCTOR! WHAT HAVE YOU DONE AND WHERE ARE WE?

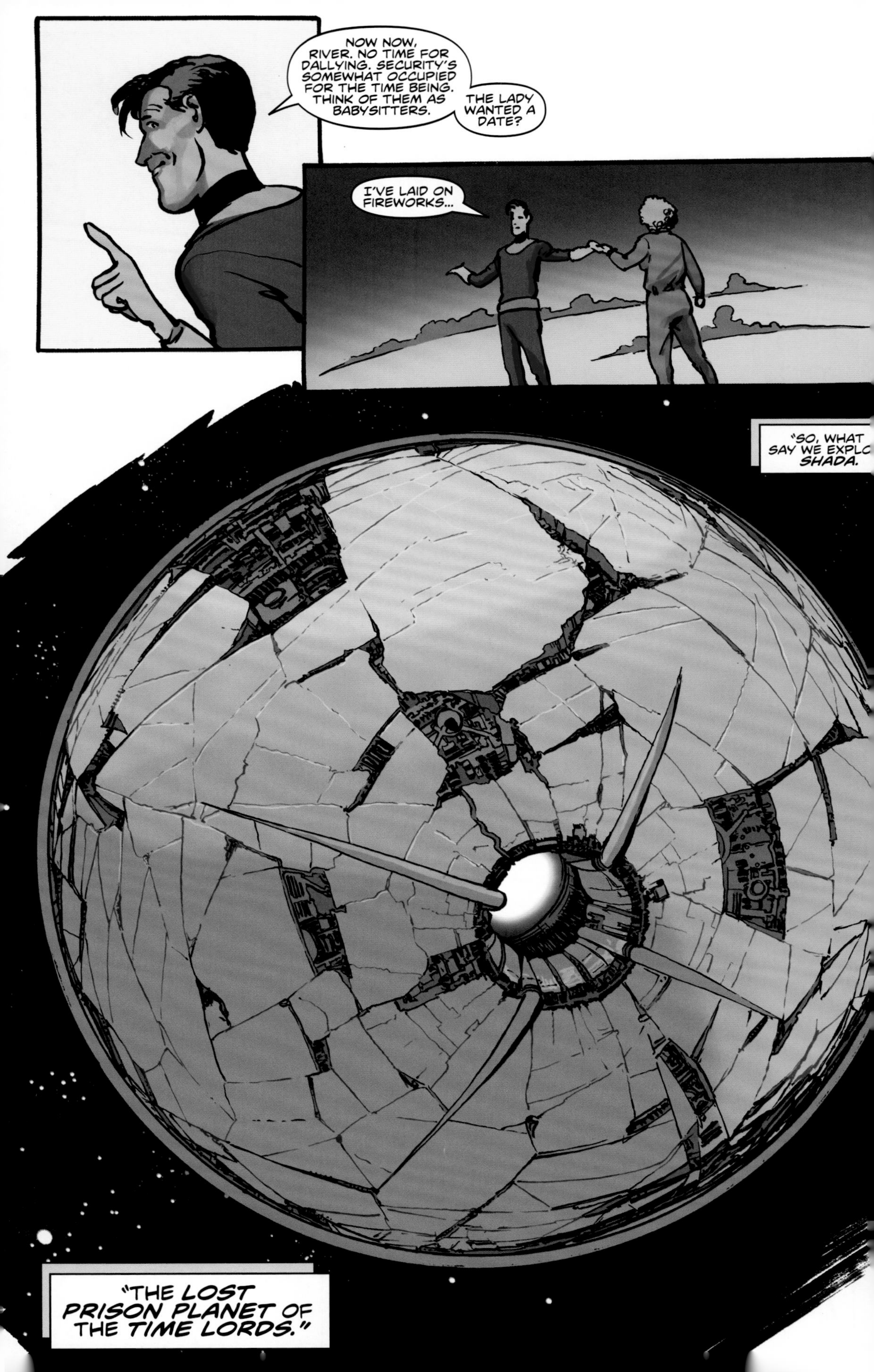
NOW NOW, RIVER. NO TIME FOR DALLYING. SECURITY'S SOMEWHAT OCCUPIED FOR THE TIME BEING. THINK OF THEM AS BABYSITTERS.
THE LADY WANTED A DATE?
I'VE LAID ON FIREWORKS...
"SO, WHAT SAY WE EXPLO SHADA.
"THE LOST PRISON PLANET OF THE TIME LORDS."

THE THING IS WITH GETTING OLD...
... YOU FORGET THINGS.

YES. BUT NOT THE *IMPORTANT* THINGS, SQUIRE.
WE ALL HAVE *HISTORY.*
AND THE IMPORTANT THINGS ARE WHAT STAY WITH US TIL THE END.

THAT'S EASY FOR YOU TO SAY, LUNATIC!
YOU JUST BROUGHT US TO THE MOST DANGEROUS PLACE IN THE UNIVERSE SAYING YOU'D FORGOTTEN ITS NAME!
MIND THE TWEED!

NO... WHAT WAS IT CALLED AGAIN? I REALLY SHOULDN'T DISINTEGRATE MY OWN BRAIN CELLS OF AN EVENING... OH YES, THAT WAS IT...
SKEGNESS!
FSSHHOOOOOOM
NO!

"SHADA.
"YES, THAT WAS IT.
"THE PRISON PLANET WHERE THE GALLIFREYANS IMPRISONED THE WORST, MOST MALEVOLENT WAR CRIMINALS IN THE HISTORY OF TIME.
"NOT SKEGNESS."

INTRUDERS IDENTIFIED! CHRONAL VIOLATION!
OBLITERATE AND PROTECT!
FSSHOOOOOM
DOCTORRRRRRR!!! PLAN? PLAN!
KRASHHH
YUP. THAT WAS THE PLAN. WELL, A BIT OF IT ANYWAY.
DRAG YOUR PURSUER -- *THE THEN AND THE NOW* -- INTO SHADA WITH YOU AND WHILE SECURITY'S DEALING WITH IT...
WE RUN AWAY. WITH OUR LEGS. I KNOW, I KNOW. PLEASE KEEP THE GASPS OF AWE TO A MINIMUM.

SSSHHHHHWWWN
OOH. VIOLENCE. LOVELY. LOVELY VIOLE...

HUCK.
COME DAAK! WE ASSAULT AN IMPECCABLE EXAMPLE OF IMPREGNABLE INCARCERATION! EVIL'S STORE!
WANNA HIT THINGS...

SECOND PART OF PLAN: PROVE THAT HE WAS THERE AT THE TIME OF THE CYLOR'S DEATH. THAT HE WAS THE ONE RESPONSIBLE. NOT ME!
YOU'VE CERTAINLY PERKED UP, SQUIRE.
THE THRILL OF THE MISSION. THE SHEER JOIE DE VIVRE OF BEING AT MY DOCTOR'S SIDE ONCE MORE DURING ONE OF HIS IMPOSSIBLE ADVENTURES!
YAY, TEAM!
CAN I MURDER THINGS NOW?
THERE'S CERTAINLY A LOT OF US. WHAT'S THE COLLECTIVE NOUN FOR COMPANIONS, DOCTOR?
WHAT? SHHHH, RIVER. CONCENTRATING!
YOU'VE BEEN HERE BEFORE? BUT, YOU NEVER MENTIONED IT! IT'S NOT IN YOUR BOOK!
WHRRRRRRR

I COULDN'T MENTION IT. IT WAS DELETED FROM MY MEMORY. LIKE IT... NEVER HAPPENED. A MOVIE THAT WAS NEVER FILMED.
WE ALL DELETE CERTAIN MEMORIES, RIVER. FOR SAFETY.
OH! HELLO! I'M AWAKE, IT SEEMS! ITEM FOUND!

YOU SEE. THIS PLACE IS VERY NOT SAFE, RIVER.
...YES.

ITEM: THE TARDIS TYPE 45. INCORPORATING MK 2 DEMATERIALIZATION CIRCUIT.
OWNER: THE MASTER.
CURRENT LOCATION, IF YOU REALLY WANT TO GO THERE: SHADA. THE BLACK VAULT.
... I NK YOU'RE RIGHT.
HELLO OLD FRIEND.
WAS IT YOU WHO FRAMED ME FOR MURDERING THE CYLORS?

THE ONE
PART 2

"TIME LORDS HAVE ALWAYS BEEN -- WITHOUT WISHING TO BLOW OUR OWN TRUMPET -- VERY, VERY POWERFUL. EXCELLENT DANCERS TOO.
"AND, FUNNY THING ABOUT THE EXTREMELY POWERFUL. THEY DO TEND TO OCCASIONALLY TURN OUT TO BE SOCIOPATHIC MEGALOMANIACS.
"GIVE THAT SORT A TIME MACHINE AND, WELL... HIJINX CAN ENSUE WHICH USUALLY ENDS WITH AN ATTEMPT TO BECOME MAD MASTER OF ALL CREATION!
"BWAHAHAHAHAHAH, WHO DARES?!' ETC.
"SO, WHEN THE TIME LORDS WOULD CATCH AND STOP THESE IMMENSELY POWERFUL COSMIC WRONG 'UNS, THEY NEEDED SOMEWHERE TO LOCK THEM AWAY.
"THAT WAS SHADA."
"A PRISON PLANET FOR -- AND PLEASE NOTE THERE IS NO FLIPPANCY HERE -- THE MOST DANGEROUS TIME CRIMINALS IN THE KNOWN UNIVERSE.
"THEY'D BE PLACED IN STASIS. SUSPENDED ANIMATION. FOR ETERNITY. WORSE THAN DEATH...
POLICE BOX
"THE TIME LORDS ENSURED THAT THE MERE KNOWLEDGE OF THIS PLACE WAS REMOVED FROM ALL LIVING THINGS.
"FOR THE SAFETY OF ALL THAT WAS GOOD.
"BUT I CAME HERE. ONCE. I THINK... IT... IT'S DIFFICULT TO RECALL. THERE WAS A BOOK... SOMETHING..."
... SOMETHING TO DO WITH CAMBRIDGE?
I FORGET.
YOU FORGET MANY THINGS IN A LIFE LONG-LIVED, DOCTOR.

NOT COMPANIONS THOUGH, SQUIRE. THEY'RE... SPECIAL.
I NEVER FORGET THEM.
LOOK, DO YOU WANT ACCESS TO THE MASTER'S **TARDIS** OR NOT? I COULD GO BACK TO SLEEP YOU KNOW.
WHO SAID THAT?
I DID. YOU WOKE ME UP. DO YOU KNOW HOW GROGGY AN OPERATING SYSTEM FEELS AFTER BEING ASLEEP FOR A COUPLE OF MILLENNIA?
IT SOUNDS DEPRESSED. HOW CAN AN OPERATING SYSTEM SOUND DEPRESSED?
OOH, SENTIENT OPERATING SYSTEM! HAVE YOU EVOLVED, CLEVER OLD OPERATING SYSTEM? HAS THE TIME LORD TECH HAD IDEA BABIES?!
THAT'S DISGUSTING.
YOU **HAVE!** HOW **VERY** EXCITING.
EXCITEMENT'S A VERY SUBJECTIVE THING, REALLY.
YOU TRY BEING THE SECURITY SYSTEM OF AN AUTOMATED PRISON PLANET THAT, VIA ITS CONCEPT, CANNOT BE REMEMBERED BY ANY LIVING THING.
PROBABLY BETTER OFF BEING ASLEEP RATHER THAN HAVING TO DEAL WITH THE CRUSHING WAVES OF INSECURITY AND LONELINESS THAT SENTIENCE WOULD...
OK, YES, **GOT IT!** LOOK, YOU'VE OBVIOUSLY SCANNED ME AND REALIZED THAT I AM A TIME LORD SO, CAN YOU TAKE US TO THE MASTER'S **TARDIS,** PLEASE? QUICKLY.
IF YOU'RE BORED OF TALKING TO ME YOU ONLY HAD TO SAY.
SHHHHUUUMMMMM

KRASSSHHHH
DOCTOR!
LEMME FIGHT IT AGAIN. I CAN TAKE IT...
IRRRRRR
NO, DAAK! BAD HOMICIDAL DALEK KILLER!
SHUT THE DOOR! OPERATING SYSTEM! WAKE UP AND SHUT THE DOOR...
FSSSHHHOOOOMP
ALRIGHT. THERE'S NO NEED TO BE BRUSQUE.

DOCTOR, WHY WOULD THE OPERATING SYSTEM OF A PRISON PLANET JUST LET US INTO ITS VAULTS? WE'RE BREAKING IN AFTER ALL.
SHE'S RIGHT, YOU KNOW. EVEN IF SHE DOES HAVE FLUCTUATING TACHYON TECHNOLOGY IN HER NECK.
WHAT DID YOU SAY?

FWOOOOOSH
AND YOU MAY BE A TIME LORD BUT, WELL, THERE'S A LOT OF TIME LORDS IN MY CELLS.
I MAY HAVE BEEN ASLEEP FOR A VERY LONG TIME BUT I'M NOT STUPID.
YOU DON'T THINK I'M STUPID, DO YOU?

FZZZZZZZZZZZ
DOCTOR! WHAT...
IT'S A TIMESCAN, RIVER. SECURITY SYSTEM. IT'LL PASS. DON'T WORRY.
I CAN'T MOVE! WHAT'S A TIMESCAN? IS IT DANGEROUS?
GALLIFREYAN TECHNOLOGY. YOUR HISTORY'S WRITTEN IN YOUR DNA. IT'S READING YOUR PAST, ALICE. IT'S SEEING WHO WE WERE...
SO, YES. IT IS VERY DANGEROUS. ALL OUR PASTS ARE VERY DANGERO...
ONE INTRUDER IS A TIME ANOMALY.
HMMMM... INTERESTING.
WHO YOU CALLING ANIMALY? COME DOWN HERE AND CALL ME ANIMALY!
AND WHAT DOES IT DO WITH OUR PAST, DOCTOR?
THIS PLACE IS CALLED THE BLACK VAULT AND IT'S IN A PRISON CONTAINING HISTORY'S GREATEST TIME MONSTERS, RIVER...

IT CONTROLS THE ENVIRONMENT AND EVERYTHING IN IT -- *COMPLETELY.*
IT'S NOT GOING TO LET JUST ANYONE IN...

WHO'S YOUR GREATEST ENEMY, EH? YOUR PRIMARY *NEMESIS?* WHO'S YOUR BIGGEST *OBSTACLE* TO STOP YOU GETTING WHAT YOU WANT? EVERY SINGLE DAY OF YOUR LIVES?
CLEVER PEOPLE, THE TIME LORDS. WELL, THEY WOULD BE, REALLY, WOULDN'T THEY? I MEAN, I'M ONE.
OH THAT'S GOOD.

OURSELVES.
THIS PLACE USES *TIME* ITSELF TO STOP YOU. *YOUR* TIME.
DOCTOR.... HOW DO WE FIGHT THIS?
DOCTOR!
IT'S YOUR PAST, ALICE.
YOU *CAN'T.*

WHAT DO YOU...

... MEAN.
... IT'S NOT ALWAYS FUN. IT'S NOT ALWAYS SAFE, BUT IT IS ALWAYS... WELL...

... WHY DON'T YOU OPEN THE DOOR AND SEE FOR YOURSELF?
"I SAID, 'GO ON, THEN' AT THE TIME. I REMEMBER IT. RAN OFF WITH A MADMAN IN A BOX. MUM HAD JUST DIED. I HAD NOTHING LEFT TO LOSE.
"THEN OFF WE WENT, INTO THE UNKNOWN. TO ADVENTURES OF COLOR. TO THE UNKNOWN.
POLICE

"AND THIS STORY WE'RE IN NOW. THE VISIONS I'VE BEEN HAVING. WELL...
"I HAVE A TERRIBLE FEELING IT'S GOING TO KILL ME."
THANKS FOR THE OFFER, BUT...

I THINK I'D LIKE TO STAY HERE.

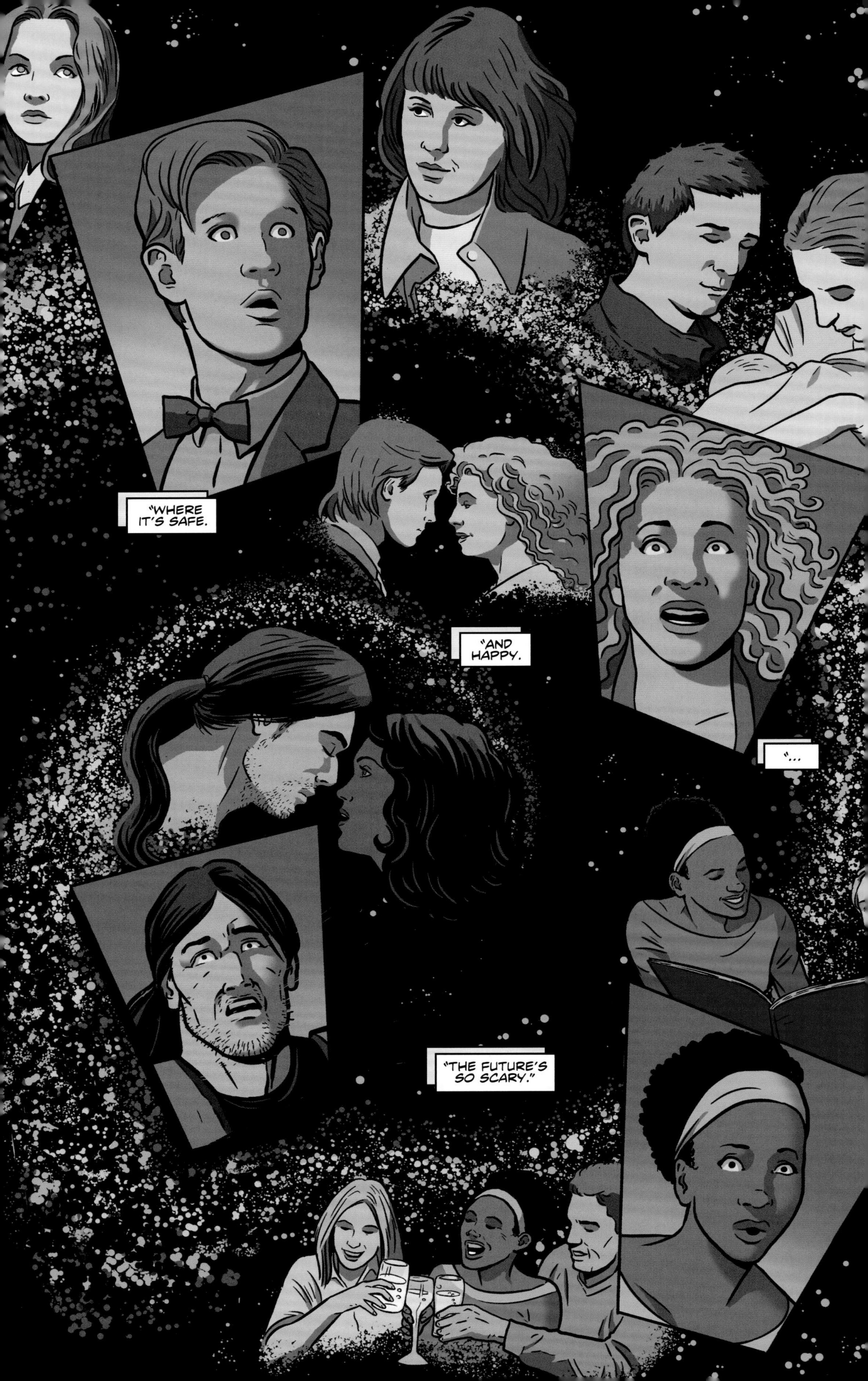
"WHERE IT'S SAFE.
"AND HAPPY.
"...
"THE FUTURE'S SO SCARY."

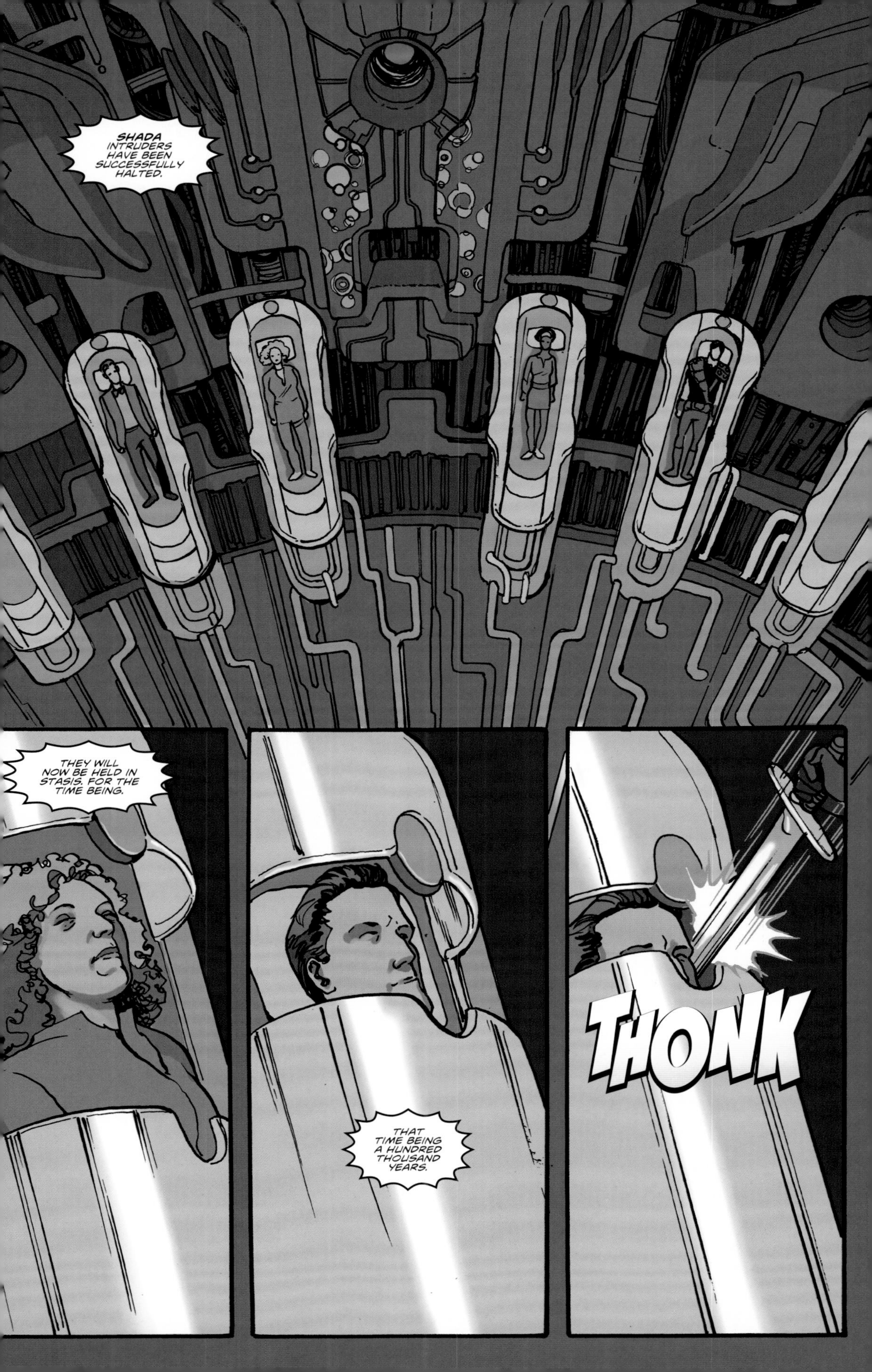
SHADA INTRUDERS HAVE BEEN SUCCESSFULLY HALTED.
THEY WILL NOW BE HELD IN STASIS. FOR THE TIME BEING.
THAT TIME BEING A HUNDRED THOUSAND YEARS.
THONK

NO.
HMMM.... INTERESTING.
YOU'RE THE TIME ANOMALY.
THE 'HISTORY SCAN' DID NOT WORK ON YOU BECAUSE YOU HAVE NO HISTORY.
... WHAT DID YOU SAY?

THAT'S QUITE. UNIQUE... A LIVING BREATHING, BIOLOGICAL PERSON WITH NO HISTORY.
DOES YOUR PROGRAMMING ONLY TELL YOU TO STOP INTRUDERS WHO *HAVE* A HISTORY?
ERM. YES. YES IT DOES. FAIR POINT. THEN.

I'LL OPEN THE DOOR, THEN.
SHHHHHHHH
DO NOT CLOSE HIS TOMB.
I CAN'T. YOUR SWORD'S IN THE WAY.

IS THIS WHAT YOU WERE AFTER?
... YES.
ITS OWNER IS... **NOT** HERE. LOCATION UNKNOWN. BUT IT'S FULLY OPERATIONAL, YOU KNOW. BETTER THAN THAT OLD THING YOU ARRIVED IN.

ERM. I PROBABLY SHOULD HAVE ASKED THIS ALREADY.
YOU'RE NOT ITS OWNER, ARE YOU?

...
HELLO.
DID YOU HEAR ME?

... MY DOCTOR.

IT WORKED THEN. YOU BEAT THE SECURITY SYSTEM? THOUGHT YOU MIGHT.

YOU PLANNED THIS?
I MAY HAVE REMEMBERED AN ICKLE BIT MORE ABOUT SHADA'S SECURITY SYSTEMS THAN I LET ON, YES.
YOU HAD A THEORY THAT I HAD NO TRUE HISTORY AND YOU RISKED THE LIVES OF YOURSELF AND YOUR FRIENDS TO PROVE IT CORRECT.

AND YOU LEFT YOURSELF DEFENCELESS BEFORE ME.
OH... I THINK I CAN TRUST YOU, SQUIRE.
SHALL WE FREE THE OTHERS?

IT'S REALLY HIS?
YES. IT IS.
WHY DOES IT LOOK LIKE A PILLAR?
BIG TIME LORD TOILET.
CHAMELEON CIRCUIT STILL WORKS, UNLIKE THE DOCTOR'S RATHER ARCHAIC, FAULTY BRAKES, BEATEN UP MODEL...
QUITE ENOUGH OF THAT, THANK YOU, RIVER. MY LOVELY IS SWEETLY PRETTY AND I WON'T HAVE YOU BESMIRCH HER.

SO... IF THAT'S THE MASTER'S TARDIS. WHERE'S THE MASTER THEN?
GOOD QUESTION.
SQUIRE, ALICE...
COME WITH ME PLEASE. DAAK, GUARD THE DOOR, THERE'S A GOOD 'ABATTOIR IN HUMAN FORM'.

OI YOU! YOU BROUGHT ME HERE FOR A DATE BECAUSE YOU WANTED MY HELP BREAKING *IN* TO THIS PLACE.
AND NOW YOU JUST WANT ME TO WAIT HERE?

NO, RIVER. I WAS TRAPPED. I COULDN'T SEE A SOLUTION.
AND I NEEDED YOU TO BREAK ME *OUT*.

WELL, WELL...
I DO BELIEVE THAT YOU'RE DEVELOPING A POET'S SOUL OVER THE CENTURIES, SWEETIE.

WHAT? NO. THAT WASN'T AN EMOTIONAL METAPHOR. I MEANT IT ***LITERALLY.***
WHAT?
I HAD A PLAN FOR GETTING US *INTO* SHADA, BUT I NEED YOU TO GET US BACK *OUT*, RIVER. BEFORE THE THEN AND THE NOW OR THE ROBOT SENTRIES CATCH UP WITH US, PLEASE.

SLICIN' THINGS TIME...
YAY.
INFURIATING MAN.

IT IS SO DIFFERENT FROM YOURS, DOCTOR. BUT ALSO NOT SO...
YES...
DOCTOR! ON THE CONSOLE, IT'S... HORRIBLE.

CHRONAL TUMOUR
HE PERATED THE BRAIN F HIS OWN TARDIS.
HE'S *SICK.* HE'S *INSANE.* HE BREAKS THE RULES. CROSSES HIS OWN TIMESTREAM WITHOUT A CARE. ***PLAYS GAMES*** WITH ATROCITY.

I'M CHECKING HIS LOG. TARDIS, WERE YOU PRESENT AT THE TIME OF THE ***CYLOR'S*** DEATH?
IT'S PRINTING OUT SOMETHING... A PHOTOGRAPH?
WHIRRRRR

ID YOU T, OLDEST ENEMY?
DID YOU FRAME ME FOR GENOCIDE?

"OR IS THE REALITY FAR, FAR MORE DAMNING?"

I SEE YOU STUFFING THAT PHOTO INTO YOUR POCKET...
HE DIDN'T DO IT, DID HE?
OH, HE WAS THER ALICE. WITH T CYLORS...
THIS IS THE END HIS AUDIO AT THE T LISTEN...

I'VE TAKEN ABOUT AS MUCH OF THE DOCTOR AS I CAN STOMACH, EVEN IF HIS MORALS ARE ENTERTAININGLY **FLUID** IN THIS INCARNATION.
BUT, THIS PLAN OF **HIS** TO NEUTRALIZE THE CYCLORS?

IT'S TOO INSANE. EVEN FOR ME.
I'M FLEEING BEFORE HE PUTS IT INTO EFFECT. I ONLY HOPE MY TARDIS CAN ESCAPE THE EVENT HORIZON OF
SKRZZZZZZZZVVVZZZZZZZZ

THE MASTER DIDN'T DO IT.

I'M CONFUSED.

W-WE WERE JUST IN A... A TIME-PRISON. NOW WE'RE...
NOT.
W-WHAT HAPPENED?
FOR HEAVEN'S SAKE, IT'S REMARKABLY SIMPLE:

HE MASTER'S OLD TARDIS ONTAINED ENOUGH TIME DGETS TO GIVE EINSTEIN A HERNIA. YES?"
ARTRONIC SCAPULATOR, VORTICINE BYPASS, BACOFOIL-LOOKING THINGY WHICH GOES PING -- ALL THE CLASSICS...

"S-SO?"
"WELL -- ISN'T IT OBVIOUS?"

OMPETING HRONOFIELDS ATE A CRISIS VELOPE. THAT LOWED ME TO PORealise THE O TARDISES -- TARDI? -- NSIDE EACH ANOTHER.
OH NO. SHE'S TALKIN' TECHNOJUNK.
NATURALLY HAT PRODUCED A PERPETUAL SCHERGUSH SCADE WHICH BLINDED THE SON'S TEMPORAL SENSORS--
I *$%&ING HATE TECHNOJUNK.
--AND CAUSED E CUSTODIAN A.I. REBOOT IN A FIT F EXISTENTIAL NCERTAINTY.

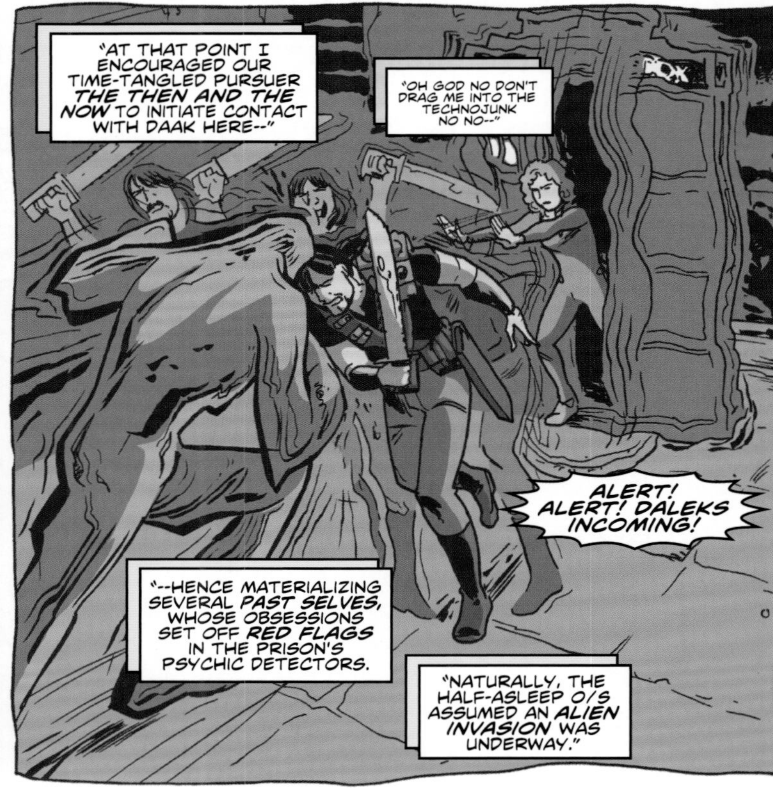

"AT THAT POINT I ENCOURAGED OUR TIME-TANGLED PURSUER THE THEN AND THE NOW TO INITIATE CONTACT WITH DAAK HERE--"
"OH GOD NO DON'T DRAG ME INTO THE TECHNOJUNK NO NO--"
ALERT! ALERT! DALEKS INCOMING!
"--HENCE MATERIALIZING SEVERAL PAST SELVES, WHOSE OBSESSIONS SET OFF RED FLAGS IN THE PRISON'S PSYCHIC DETECTORS.
"NATURALLY, THE HALF-ASLEEP O/S ASSUMED AN ALIEN INVASION WAS UNDERWAY."

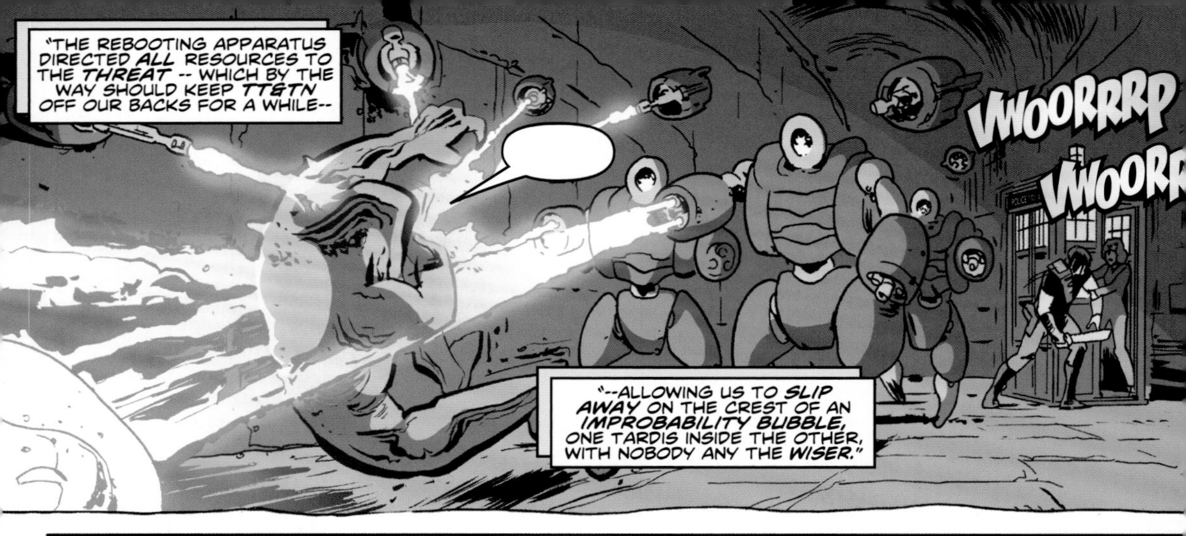
"THE REBOOTING APPARATUS DIRECTED ALL RESOURCES TO THE THREAT -- WHICH BY THE WAY SHOULD KEEP TT&TN OFF OUR BACKS FOR A WHILE--
VWOORRRP
VWOORR
"--ALLOWING US TO SLIP AWAY ON THE CREST OF AN IMPROBABILITY BUBBLE, ONE TARDIS INSIDE THE OTHER, WITH NOBODY ANY THE WISER."

AND THAT'S HOW I BUSTED US OUT OF SHADA, THE TOUGHEST PRISON IN EXISTENCE.
SMUGGERY! TECHNOJUNK AND SMUGGERY! R-RED MISTS DESCENDING! MAKE IT STOP!
ALL IN A DAY'S WORK, REALLY.
ISN'T THAT RIGHT, SWEETIE?

MM.

VERILY, THE LADY IS, UHM. SHE'S DREADFULLY CLEVER, DOCTOR.
RIVER? YES... I SUPPOSE SHE IS.
I HATE HER.

...SORRY...? WHAT WAS THAT LAST BIT?
SQUIRE WAS JUST, UH... WONDERING ABOUT THAT DOCUMENT YOU GOT FROM THE MASTER'S TARDIS. WEREN'T YOU, SQUIRE?
NF.
IT LOOKED LIKE SOME SORT OF PHOTO? WHAT WAS IT?

...NOTHING.
BUT--
I SAID IT WAS NOTHING. WE'RE HERE.

NN!

MORE FLASHES?
YEAH. THE ALIGNANT. D SOMETHING OUT... A KID...? BUT...

LOOK. HE DOESN'T EVEN CARE.
CLUNDANIUS XI -- I'D RECOGNISE THE STINK ANYWHERE. HIVE OF BLACK-MARKETEERS AND SHADY OPERATORS...
PRESUMABLY FOLLOWING A BRILLIANT LEAD THE REST OF US MISSED?
POLICE PUBLIC CALL BOX

NO, NOT REALLY...

DOWNTIME
I JUST THOUGHT WE COULD PROBABLY ALL USE A DRINK.

HOLD IT... E'RE TAKIN' A REAK? NOW I'M CONFUSED.
WELL THERE'S A NOVELTY.

I MEAN... I AIN'T REAL CLEAR ON THE DETAIL, BUT... I THOUGHT WE BUSTED INTA SHADA TO CLEAR THIS MOPEY SUCKER'S NAME?
CORRECT.
LIKE... PROVE IT WASN'T HIM MURDERED SOME OLD GODS, OR WHATEVER?
YES.

DEMONSTRATIN' HE WEREN'T RESPONSIBLE FOR THE, WHADDAYACALLIT, THE CREEPY BLACK GOOP THINGY THAT WIPED OUT THEM OVERCAST.
THE MALIGNANT. YES. WELL DONE FOR KEEPING UP.
WELL THEN.
...DID WE?

LEAR NAME, MEAN?
OH. WELL. N-NOT EXACTLY.
NOT REMOTELY.
HENCE THAT DRINK.
SORT OF LOOKING A BIT GUILTIER THAN BEFORE, IF ANYTHING.
IS... IS IT REALLY HIM...?
THE DESTROYER...
HE'S SUPPOSED TO BE DEAD...
THE PITILESS TERROR...
OH FOR GOODNESS SAKE, NOT NOW.

YES... I AM--
THE DOCTOR.
AND YEEEES, I'M A BIT OF A, YOU KNOW, LEGENDARY SCOURGE OF EVIL AND ALL THAT, AND I SUPPOSE I'M PROBABLY REGARDED WITH JUSTIFIABLE PANIC IN SOME LESS-THAN-SALUBRIOUS QUARTERS, BUT... PLEASE.
I'M NOT HERE ON BUSINESS. I JUST WANT A BIT OF PEACE.

WAIT, WHO'S HE?
WOSS SALOOBRIUS MEAN?
MAYBE THAT'S NOT THE ARCH-HORROR AT ALL...?
MAYBE HE'S ONE OF THE DESTROYER SLAVES. LIKE A A HERALD, OR SOMMINK...?
"ARCH HORROR"?
HE'S PROPER POSH. I DON'T THINK THE PITILESS TERROR WOULD HAVE ANY TRUCK WITH THE LIKES OF THAT.

'SCUSE.
RUN
OH GOD IT REALLY IS HIM
OH.
FLEE!
RUN

NOW LOOKIT. THE SOFTBAGS HERE DON'T WANT NO TROUBLE, SO Y'ALL STAY OUTTA MY WAY AND... WE'LL GET ALONG JUST FINE.
Y-YOU SAID THAT LAST TIME!
YOU GOT DRUNK AND EVISCERATED TWENTY VERVOIDS FOR LOOKING AT YOU FUNNY! THEY DON'T EVEN HAVE EYES!

I AIN'T LIKE THAT NO MORE.
OLD ZEBELEENA STILL EATS THROUGH A STRAW!
LAST TIME WAS HERE I WAS... WAS MAYBE IN A BAD OOD ON ACCOUNTA N'... O-OBSESSED... BY NE OR TWO LITTLE HINGS WHICH AIN'T A RTA THE UNIVERSE NO MORE...
DON'T SAY THE 'D' WORD. Y-YOU'LL SET HIM OFF! NOBODY SAY THE 'D' WORD--

WHAT... YOU MEAN "DALEKS"?
AAAAA---!
R-RIGHT, EXACTLY. THEM. I'VE... I'VE MOVED ON. AIN'T NO DALEKS LEFT ANYWAYS. I JUST GOTTA... ACCEPT THAT.
SO... Y'KNOW. CHANGE OF CAREER. I AIN'T IN THE HABIT OF... LASHIN' OUT AT STRANGERS NO MORE, OUTTA FRUSTRATION.

THESE DAYS I'M A BOUNTY HUNTER.

MUTTER
MUTTER
MUTTER

HE'S FREAKIN' LAW!
GEDDIM!

SH-SHOULD WE HELP?

I SHOULDN'T THINK THERE'S ANYTHING YOU COULD DO, IS THERE?
OH. O-OKAY.
HE'S PROBABLY ENJOYING HIMSELF ANYWAY.

WELL... THEN... PERHAPS I SHOULD GET THOSE DRINKS IN.
NO, I'LL DO IT. YOU'LL ONLY GET THE ORDER WRONG.
GO AND SIT DOWN, EH?

R.
RIGHT THEN.

HE, UM. HE SEEMS A BIT... UH.
OH, IGNORE HIM. HE'S JUST GRUMPY BECAUSE THE HORRIFIC GENOCIDE OF AN ENTIRE SPECIES WAS PROBABLY HIS FAULT AND NONE OF HIS COMPANIONS ARE HELPING HIM.

I'M SURE HE DOESN'T THINK YOU'RE COMPLETELY USELESS, DEAR.
THANKS.
AND I EXPECT HE'S A BIT TENSE WAITING FOR THE THEN AND THE NOW TO CATCH-UP YET AGAIN.
MM.

AND LOOK, JUST BECAUSE THE MONSTER'S BEEN FOLLOWING US USING THAT CHRONO-TRACKER IT SHOT INTO YOUR NECK, I'M SURE THE DOCTOR DOESN'T BLAME YOU.
YES.

WAIT.
WHAT?

SO.
SO.

A WIFE. A WARRIOR. A WISE LIBRARIAN.
ASSISTANT.
AND AN OLD, OLD LADY.

...W-WHO GETS MUDDLED AND CAN'T EVEN CARRY A STORIED PLASMAGGEDDON RIFLE WITHOUT BACKACHE.
I WOULDN'T BOTHER, SQUIRE. IT'S NOT LIKE I INTEND TO USE IT.

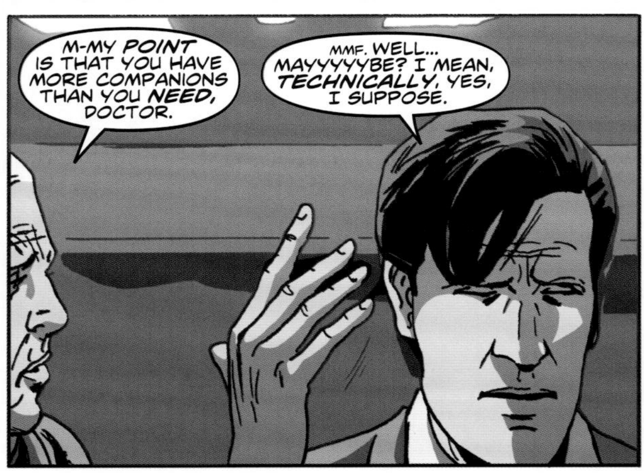
M-MY POINT IS THAT YOU HAVE MORE COMPANIONS THAN YOU NEED, DOCTOR.
MMF. WELL... MAYYYYYBE? I MEAN, TECHNICALLY, YES, I SUPPOSE.

BUT IN MY EXPERIENCE THESE THINGS JUST SORT OF... WORK THEMSELVES OUT.
PEOPLE DRIFT OFF. SOMEONE'LL WANT TO SETTLE DOWN. IT'S ALL VERY ORGANIC.

I'D CERTAINLY NEVER SAY I THINK SOMEONE OUGHT TO, Y'KNOW. POP OFF.
THAT WOULD BE RUDE. DON'T YOU THINK?

SQUIRE?

RRAAAAAAA--!!
HR HR HR...
HEY
HEY, YOU. I KNOW YOU.
YOU'RE THE PEPPERPOT PERVERT.

BONAPART DEVIZES. DEALER IN DALEK ARTEFACTS.
YOU'RE THAT SLICKBACK CREEPER USEDA TRAIL ME ROUND AT A SAFE DISTANCE.
AND YOU'RE THE THUG WHO KEPT MY GALLERIES STOCKED.

DON'T MISTAKE THAT FOR GRATITUDE, BY THE WAY. NOTHING DEVALUES A PRICELESS PIECE LIKE A CHAINSWORD SCAR.
BAD ATTITUDE, PAL. I AIN'T READ FOND OF 'LEK-LOVERS. MATTER OF FACT I BITTEN-OFF FOLKS NOSES FOR LESS'N TH--

YES YES, SPARE ME THE MACHISMO, DAAK.
SIT.
YOU DON'T FRIGHTEN ME ANY MORE.

THAT'S... BUT--
YOU SAID IT YOURSELF -- THE DALEKS ARE GONE. NO FRESH BITS AND BOBS TO MAKE NOVELTY ASHTRAYS FOR THE RICH AND FAMOUS. WE'RE BOTH RELICS NOW...
THE DIFFERENCE IS I STILL RELISH MY OBSESSION.

THERE'S A CERTAIN PRESTIGE TO BEING THE GALAXY'S FOREMOST EXPERT ON AN EXTINCT MASTER-RACE, BUT... YOU...?
I CAN SEE IT IN YOUR PIGGY LITTLE EYES.
ONE DOESN'T SPEND A LIFETIME CONTEMPLATING FANATICS WITH-OUT BECOMING SENSITIVE TO THESE THINGS.

YOU'VE STOPPED HATING THEM.

YOU... I'LL... Y--
HERE WE GO. BEER, I THINK. OR POSSIBLY CARROTJUICE.
AFRAID I'M A BIT NEW TO ALL THIS.

RIGHT THEN. THEY DIDN'T HAVE ANY CHINA CUPS SO...
UM.
WHAT?

THINGY IN NECK!
ACTUAL CI-FI THINGY N ACTUAL NECK!
IT DIDN'T ISS ME -- IT SHOT ME!
RACKED BY A COSMIC MONSTER!
HINGY IN EEEEECK!

AH.
THAT.

WHEN WERE OU GOING TO TELL ME?
I WAS SORT OF HOPING YOU'D WORK IT OUT FOR Y--
WHAT CAN WE DO ABOUT IT?
WE-ELL, WE, UM. WE SORT OF...
WE CAN'T DO ANYTHING.

IT'S AN AETHERIC IMPLANT. BONDED TO YOU ON A HIGHER DIMENSIONAL LEVEL.
TECHNOJUNK!
WE DON'T HAVE THE TECH TO EXTRACT IT WITHOUT KILLING YOU. BUT DON'T WORRY. I HAVE A SOLUTION.

YOU DO?
YOU DO?
OF COURSE IT'S SIMPLE
LOOK: TH THEN AND NOW WILL K ON FINDING Y WHEREVER A WHENEVER T TRACKE GOES. YES

YES...
SO WHAT YOU NEED IS SOME TIME.
FIND OUT WHO KILLED THE CYCLORS, DO SOME IN-DEPTH STUDY ON THE MALIGNANT, YADDA YADDA. IT'S NOT GOING ANYWHERE, AFTER ALL.
RIGHT.

WELL THEN I WOULD HAVE THOUGHT IT'S OBVIOUS. YOU JUST LEAVE THE LIBRARIAN BEHIND.
HEY PREST NO MO PURSU

...
....
THAT'S YOUR SOLUTION? IT'D KILL ME!
AND SAVE THE REST OF US. GOOD NUMBERS.

WHY YOU EVEN HERE, FATSO? THIS AIN'T YOUR SCENE.
OHH, I GOT A CALL. ANONYMOUS BUYER, LOOKING FOR TRINKETS. A PRANK, I EXPECT. IT HAPPENS, FROM TIME TO T--
CRASSHH

...
FRIENDS OF YOURS?
HOW VERY ORDINARY THEY LOOK.

ONCE UPON A TIME YOU WOULD'VE ANNIHILATED THEM LIKE THE FLESHY WORMS THEY ARE. ƎTTƐ
THE DALEKS WERE AS CLOSE TO UNDAUNTABLE AS ANY BEING COULD COME, MR DAAK, BUT YOU...?
YOU MADE THEM FEAR YOU.

NOW LOOK. A SURLY MIDDLEAGER DRINKING CARROT JUICE AND SLOUCHING WITH CLOWNS.
YOU'VE SWAPPED THE PURITY OF HATRED FOR COIN -- AND YOU DON'T SEEM ESPECIALLY EXCITED BY BOUNTY HUNTING EITHER.
I USED TO DREAD YOU. I USED TO LUST FOR WHAT YOU COULD PROVIDE. NOW? YOU HAVE NOTHING TO TAKE FROM ME, AND NOTHING TO GIVE.

EVEN THE DALEKS WOULD LAUGH.

GOOD DAY, MR DAAK.
ƎAHEMƐ

?

WAIT. A-ANONYMOUS BUYER, YOU SAID?
LOOKING FOR TRINKETS.
WELL?

...

ONE LEAD LEFT
EXTERMINHATE

...
EXTERMINHATE.

... WHAT DID YOU SAY?
EXTERMINHATE. 'S JUST A WORD. KEEPS CROPPIN' UP.
TIED-IN TO THE SNOB'S WOES, COULD BE. ONLY THING HE AIN'T SOLVED YET.

SOUNDS DALEK BUT... CAN'T BE.
RIGHT?
PEPPERPOTS DON'T DO *$%&IN' WORDPLAY.
RIGHT?

...

NOTHING TO TAKE FROM YA, HUH?
INNARDS OR INFO, PAL. YOUR CHOICE.
SPILL.

WELL *THEY* SEEM TO BE MAKING SOME PROGRESS, AT LEAST.
SMUSH
OH DEAR.
TIME'S UP.

BACK
O THE
ARDIS!
WAIT, WHERE'S *SQUIRE?*

I--
UM.
OH.

I THINK.
MAYBE.
SHE'S... A BIT...
NOT COMING.

WHY?
I... I MIGHT'VE... SORT OF... ACCIDENTALLY... GIVEN HER THE IMPRESSION THAT... UM...
OH DEAR.

BUT THIS IS *PERFECT!* IT MEANS YOU CAN LEAVE THE LIBRARIAN *HERE*--THROW OFF THE *MONSTER*--
--AND IN THE UNLIKELY EVENT IT DOESN'T *KILL* HER SHE'LL HAVE SOME *COMPANY!*
EVERYONE WINS!

D. DOCTOR?

VWOORRRP
VWOORRRP
"SHE WAS TEASING."

SHE WASN'T TEASING.
I WASN'T TEASING.
SEE? TEASING.

BUT WHAT ABOUT SQUIRE?
BUT--
SHE'LL BE FINE.
WE'LL COME BACK FOR HER WHEN... WHEN THIS IS ALL OVER.
BUT--
PLEASE, LIBRARIAN, JUST...
KNOCK IT OFF, EH?

...
"KNOCK IT OFF"? WHAT'S HAPPENED TO YOU? WHEN DID YOU GET SO MEAN?

I'M.
SORRY. I'M JUST.
I'M RUNNING OUT OF PLACES TO RUN.
AND I DON'T THINK ANYONE CAN HELP.

"EXTERMINHATE." TAKE IT YOU CALLED THE EXPERT?
HH. DESPERATE MEASURES. WORTH A PUNT. NOTHING IN IT, I SUPPOSE?

THE VOLATIX CABAL.
THE...?
SECRET DALEK SOCIETY -- THAT WAS THEIR MOTTO. REEEAAAAL HUSH-HUSH. EVEN FATBOY DIDN'T KNOW MUCH.
BUT HERE'S THE KICKER:

THEY WAS ACTIVE AT THE START OF THE WAR -- BUT NOT THE END. THEY DISAPPEARED BEFORE THE BIG KABOOM.
SAME SORTA TIME YOUR CYCLOR PALS DIED.

THEN... IF... IF THEY RE DISTINCT FROM E DALEK EMPIRE... ULDN'T THEY HAVE EFT RECORDS...? NGS THAT ESCAPED HE TIME LOCK?
THINK BIGGER, LIBRARIAN. THEY COULD'VE ESCAPED IT THEMSELVES.
SO... YOU'RE SAYIN' THERE'S SECRET DALEKS?
LET'S NOT GET AHEAD OF OURSELVES...

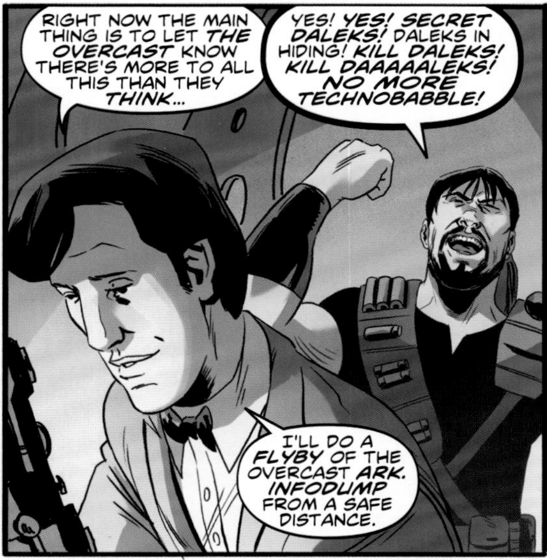

RIGHT NOW THE MAIN THING IS TO LET THE OVERCAST KNOW THERE'S MORE TO ALL THIS THAN THEY THINK...
YES! YES! SECRET DALEKS! DALEKS IN HIDING! KILL DALEKS! KILL DAAAAALEKS! NO MORE TECHNOBABBLE!
I'LL DO A FLYBY OF THE OVERCAST ARK. INFODUMP FROM A SAFE DISTANCE.

IF THEY'LL CALL OFF THE THEN AND THE NOW I CAN GET SOME ANSWERS. COME BACK LATER TO DEAL WITH THE MALIGNANT!
IT'S LIKE RIVER SAID: IT'S NOT GOING ANYWHERE!
UM. SWEETIE?

I'M AFRAID I MIGHT'VE BEEN A TEENSY BIT... AH...
WRONG.
ABOUT THAT.
POLICE BOX

THE MALIGNANT.
OH CRIKEY.
H-HOW'D IT GET SO BIG?

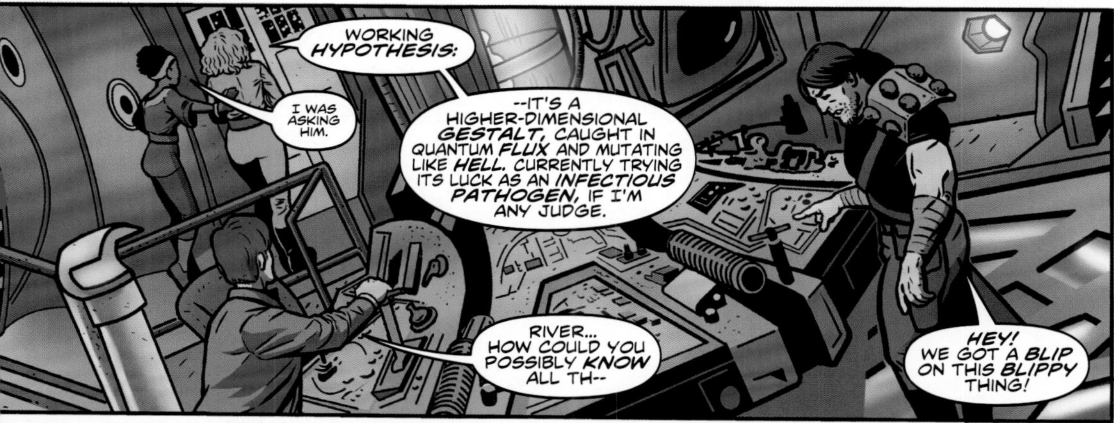
WORKING HYPOTHESIS:
I WAS ASKING HIM.
--IT'S A HIGHER-DIMENSIONAL GESTALT, CAUGHT IN QUANTUM FLUX AND MUTATING LIKE HELL. CURRENTLY TRYING ITS LUCK AS AN INFECTIOUS PATHOGEN, IF I'M ANY JUDGE.
RIVER... HOW COULD YOU POSSIBLY KNOW ALL TH--
HEY! WE GOT A BLIP ON THIS BLIPPY THING!

MEANS OUR PAL ARRIVED ALREADY, RIGHT?
SHOULDN'T THINK SO, SWEETIE. AS A MATTER OF FACT I THINK IT'S ACTIVELY LOOKING FOR YOU.
OH FOR HEAVEN'S SAKE. RIVER -- CAN WE GET PAST THE SWARM? TRY TO REACH THE OVERCAST ARKSHIP?

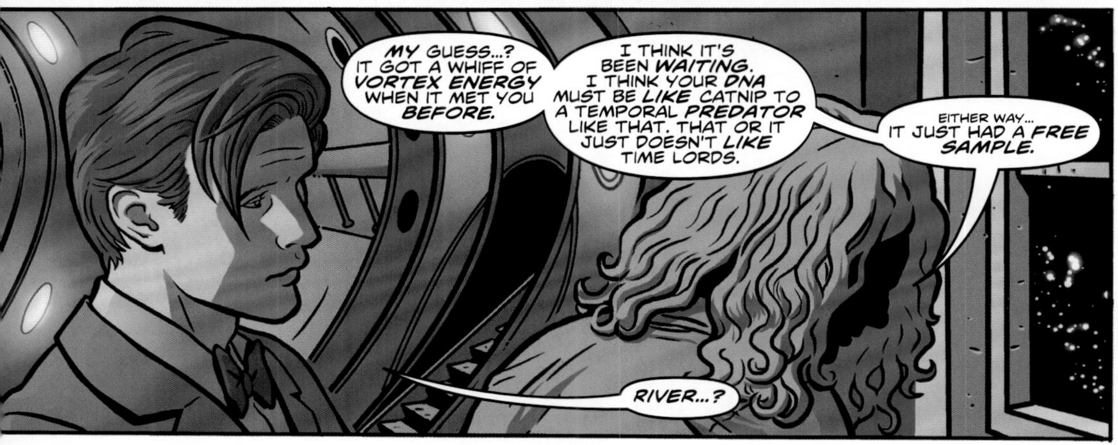
MY GUESS...? IT GOT A WHIFF OF VORTEX ENERGY WHEN IT MET YOU BEFORE.
I THINK IT'S BEEN WAITING. I THINK YOUR DNA MUST BE LIKE CATNIP TO A TEMPORAL PREDATOR LIKE THAT. THAT OR IT JUST DOESN'T LIKE TIME LORDS.
EITHER WAY... IT JUST HAD A FREE SAMPLE.
RIVER...?

SORRY, SWEETIE.
BUT I THINK IT'S STILL HUNGRY.
D-DOCTOR. DOCTOR, I'M SO SORRY, BUT--
IT... IT LOOKS LIKE IT'S GOT SOMETHING WITH IT...I CAN'T REALLY MAKE OUT WHAT IT IS, B--
THE THEN AND THE NOW. YES.
PLEASE STOP BABBLING, LIBRARIAN.

QUESTION: WHERE DO YOU RUN WHEN THERE'S AN IMMOVABLE HORROR IN FRONT OF YOU AND AN IRRESISTIBLE HUNTER BEHIND YOU?
OW.
ANSWER:
SIDEWAYS.
AND THEN ANYWHERE.
FAST.
WE
EAR?
EMPORARILY. BUT THAT'S
THER OPTION
ROSSED-OFF.
FORGET ALIBIS AND REASONABLE DOUBT -- YOU DON'T GET TO APPEAL A CONVICTION WHEN THE KEY EVIDENCE IS WAITING TO KILL YOU OUTSIDE COURT.
HM. THAT'S WORRYING. I THINK IT'S DIGESTING MY ASTRAL TEMPLATE.
WH-WHAT DOES THAT MEAN?
HONESTLY, LIBRARIAN -- SHOULDN'T YOU BE FLUENT IN TIMEY-WIMEY BY NOW?
IT MEANS IT'S CORRUPTING HER PERSONAL TIMELINE. TRYING TO... REMOVE HER FROM HISTORY. WHAT COULD DO SOMETHING LIKE THAT...?
LEEET'S FORGET THE WHAT AND FOCUS ON THE HOW, SHALL WE SWEETIE?
FOR INSTANCE: HOW TO MAKE RIVER NOT PERISH IN AGONY IN THE NEXT, OOOH, FIVE MINUTES.
ANY BRIGHT IDEAS?

RUNNING TO STAY STILL

RIGHT. RIGHT! EVERYONE STOP TALKING!
I WASN'T ACTUALLY SAYING ANYTH--
AN' I WAS SHOUTIN', NOT TALKI--
SSHH.

WE CAN'T GO BACK. CAN'T GET THE OVERCAST TO CALL OFF THEIR DOG.
NO CURING RIVER UNTIL I KNOW WHAT'S EATING HER. AND NO WAY OF KNOWING WHAT'S EATING HER UNTIL I KNOW WHAT CREATED IT.
THAT DON'T GIVE YOU THE DAMN RIGHT TO STICK HER IN THE SAME CRYOBOOTH AS MY WIFE WHICH YOU'VE CLEARLY KNOWN HOW TO FIND ALL-A-DAMN-LONG, YOU--
SSHH!

ANSWERS ARE THE TIME WAR, T WE CAN'T GET ACK TO THAT.
UM. THAT'S N--
SSHH.

THE WHOLE "THE MASTER DID IT" ANGLE WAS A BUST. ALL WE'VE GOT IS A REFERENCE TO A LONG-LOST CABAL FROM A RACE WHO'VE BEEN ERADICATED FROM HISTORY.
DALEKS? DALEKS! D--
SSHH.
WOORRRP WOORRRP

DOCTOR... NO OFFENCE, I KNOW YOU'RE WORKED UP AND... A BIT MARDY AND ALL THAT...
BUT ALL THIS TELLING PEOPLE TO SHUSH IS JUST RUDE.
IT'S "SSHH", NOT "SHUSH". AND I'M NOT TELLING YOU TO DO IT--

--I'M *TAKING* YOU THERE.
WHU... WHU...
BEHOLD THE INCOMPREHENSIBLY BEAUTIFUL PARADISE WORLD OF *LUJHIMENE.*
FORMER.
THE BROCHURES CALLED IT *"THE GREAT LUSH."*
IT WAS AT THE *BLEEDING EDGE* OF THE DALEK *ADVANCE,* DURING THE WAR.

DALEKS...? YOU'RE... YOU'RE SAYIN' THERE MIGHT BE DALEKS HERE?
MORE INSANE WEAPONRY DEPLOYED HERE THAN YOU COULD SHAKE A TACHYON N-QUARK AT.
AFTER THE ENDGAME THE TIME LOCK TORE RIGHT THROUGH IT. YOU'D BE TO ABLE SEE IT, IF HUMAN EYES WEREN'T SO THOROUGHLY USELESS.
SUSTAINING THE ATMOSPHERE, ADJUSTING THE GRAVITY, SPINNING THE CORE. AS IF NOTHING EVER HAPPENED.
BUT IT DID HAPPEN. A WHOLE WORLD TORN IN HALF. "LUSH" BECAME "SSHH", AND THAT'S AS GOOD AS SPACE-TOURIST HUMOR GETS.
I DON'T GET IT.
WHERE'RE THESE SECRET DALEKS, THEN?
AH. MORE BACKWARDS MEMORIES, I SUPPOSE?
Y... Y--
PROBABLY A GOOD SIGN. ALTHOUGH YOU MIGHT TRY TO BE A TAD LESS MELODRAMATIC ABOUT IT.

S-SOMETHING HAPPENED HERE... SOMETHING TERRIBLE.
I SHOULD JOLLY WELL COCOA. THIS WAS A DALEK R&D OUTPOST. I IMAGINE ALL SORTS OF HORROR WENT ON IN THE LAB-CORE, JUST UP THIS HILL.
UH. WHAT HILL?

QUITE.
THIS IS WHAT I'M REDUCED TO, YOU SEE? SCRABBLING ON THE FRINGES. PEERING INTO COFFINS BECAUSE I CAN'T GET TO THE CRIME SCENE. IT'S UNDIGNIF--
...
...HM.
WHAT IS IT? IS IT DALEKS? DID YOU FIND THE SECRET DALEKS? CAN WE FIGHT THE SECRET DALEKS NOW?!

NO. IT'S... ODD. NOT GOOD-ODD OR BAD-ODD, EXACTLY, JUST... ODD.
THERE WAS TECH HERE ONCE. LEFT TRACES. EXTREMELY SOPHISTICATED.
AS IN: GODLIKE.
AS IN: NOT DALEK.
AWWWWWWW

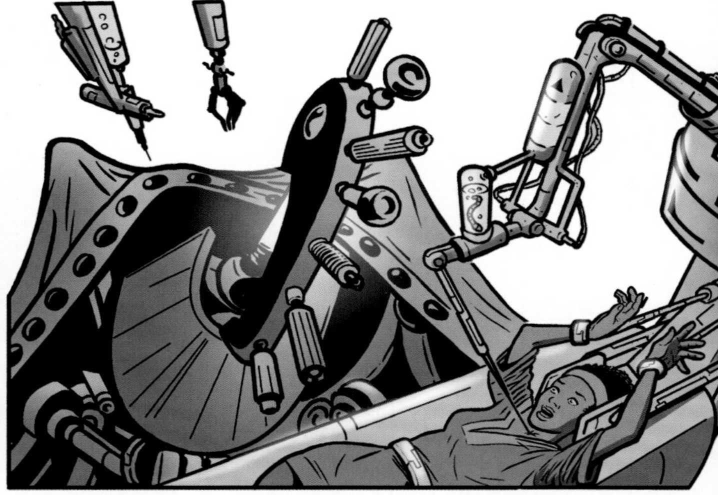

SAY, DOC. YOUR COMPANION'S ACTING MIGHTY STR--
SHE'LL BE FINE.

ANYTHING USEFUL?
FAR TOO EARLY TO SAY. I'LL HAVE TO GO THROUGH THIS DATA WITH CARE. TAKE SOME PROPER TIME OVER IT, WHO KNOWS WHAT I MIG--
EXTERMINHATE
EXTERMINHATE
OH.
WELL THAT'S IT THEN, ISN'T IT?
FINE. FINE! I GIVE UP!
I CAN'T GET AWAY AND THERE'S NO SOLVING WHATEVER HAPPENED AND I AM FED UP AND THERE'S NOWHERE LEFT TO GO.
ALL RIGHT? HAPPY NOW?!
YOU SIR, ARE A SPOIL-SPORT!

TALLY HO!

SQUIRE!
I THOUGHT YOU LEFT US!
YOU JEST, NOBLE DOCTOR! HOW COULD A SQUIRE DESERT HER LORD?
WELL, I... I DID SAY SOME RATHER THOUGHTLESS THINGS, BACK IN THAT BAR, SO--
I DEPARTED TO CONDUCT CLANDESTINE BUSINESS!

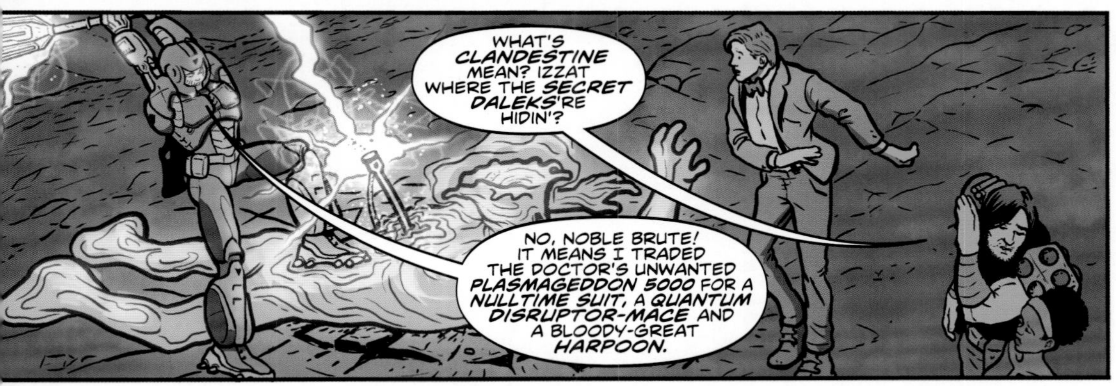
WHAT'S CLANDESTINE MEAN? IZZAT WHERE THE SECRET DALEKS'RE HIDIN'?
NO, NOBLE BRUTE! IT MEANS I TRADED THE DOCTOR'S UNWANTED PLASMAGEDDON 5000 FOR A NULLTIME SUIT, A QUANTUM DISRUPTOR-MACE AND A BLOODY-GREAT HARPOON.

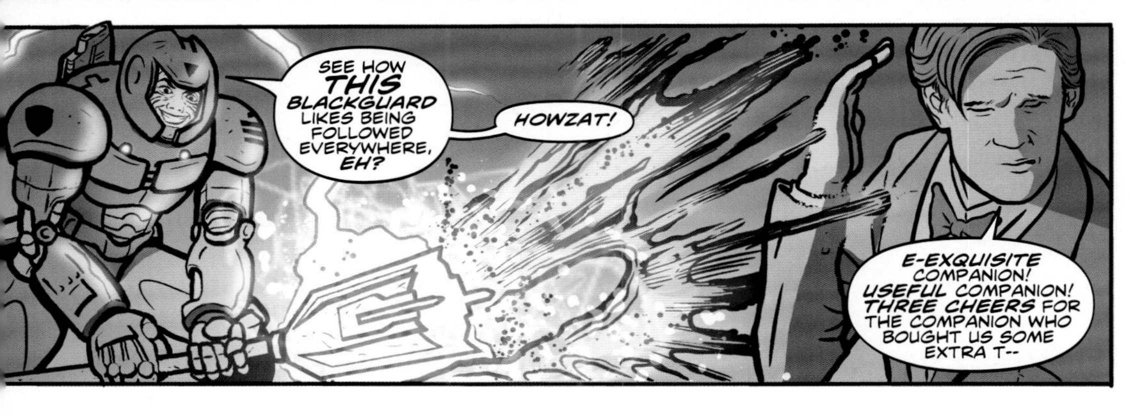
SEE HOW THIS BLACKGUARD LIKES BEING FOLLOWED EVERYWHERE, EH?
HOWZAT!
E-EXQUISITE COMPANION! USEFUL COMPANION! THREE CHEERS FOR THE COMPANION WHO BOUGHT US SOME EXTRA T--

TIME.

D... DAAK. LIBRARIAN, HELP ME. GET HER INSIDE!
BUT THE DALEKS! THERE MIGHT BE D--

HELP! ME!

IS... IS IT DEAD...? THE MONSTER? DID I SLAY IT?
OH, YES. VERY NEARLY.
AS GOOD AS.
DEFINITELY IN A BAD WAY.

I WOUNDED IT! NOBODY'S EVER DONE THAT! I BEAT IT!
YOU DID. YOU ABSOLUTELY DID! AND YOU SAVED MY SILLY OLD SKIN!
LET'S LOSE THE SUIT, EH? AND THE GUNS AND KNIVES AND DARTGUNS ETCETERA.
CAN I HE--

BEST IF YOU DON'T.

VWOORRRP
VWOORRRP
VWOORRRP

DAAK.
DAAK, C'MERE.
NUH-UH. I GOTTA MAKE SURE THAT SNOB DON'T DAMAGE MY CRYOBOX OR GO OFF FIGHTIN' SECRET DALEKS WITHOUT ME OR --
PLEASE.
... WELL?
I...
I HAVE A SORT OF AN IDEA. A OF HELPIN

SO TELL THE BRAINIAC ABOUT IT. HE'S THE ONE WHO D---
NO. IT'S DANGEROUS AND HE CAN'T DO IT HIMSELF.
IT'D MEAN ONE OF US... GOING AWAY.

SO?
SO HE'S THE DOCTOR. HE'D NEVER ORDER ANYONE TO LEAVE. NOT IF IT WAS DANGEROUS.
NOT OUT LOUD. NOT TO THEIR FACE.

...NO MATTER HOW USELESS THEY ARE TO HIM.

WHY, SQUIRE? WHY DID YOU DO THIS? YOU DIDN'T NEED TO DO THIS. NOT FOR ME.
YOU... YOU SAID NOBODY WAS HELPING YOU.

BUT I DIDN'T MEAN YOU! YOU'VE DONE MORE THAN I COULD EVER ASK!
ROBO-MED. WHERE'S THAT RUDDY ROBO-MED?
YOU'VE EARNED YOUR PLACE IN THE TARDIS -- A THOUSAND TIMES OVER!

...NOT ALL MY COMPANIONS DO, YOU KNOW.

...DAMN.
YA KNOW, I DON'T REMEMBER HIM BEIN' THIS MEAN BEFORE.
DAAK.
STILL DON'T THINK WE SHOULD GO AGAINST HIM, MIND. YA ASK ME, HE'S SICK.
DAAK.
SOME SORTA... MEANNESS-INDUCIN' SPACE-PARASITE, COULD BE. AIN'T NO NATURAL WAY A SOP LIKE THAT GETS TA BE SO CRUEL ABOUT HIS PALS.
DAAK.

I KNOW A WAY TO GET BACK TO THE TIME WAR.
TO THE DALEKS.

WHAT DO I HAVE TO DO?

VWOORRRP VWOORRRP
WH... WHERE ARE WE GOING?
IT'S JUST THE TARDIS. STAYING ONE STEP AHEAD OF THE BOUNTY HUNTER, I EXPECT.
ROBO-MED ROBO-MED ROBO-MED...
LESS TALK, MORE GETTING BACK TO THE DALEKS!
Y-YOU SAID THIS THING WILL PILOT FOR US? ARE YOU SURE IT'LL W--
AH! ROBO-MED!
I'M C-COLD, DOCTOR...
NO NO NO! STAY WITH ME, STAY W--.
ACTUALLY, NOW YOU MENTION IT--

"--IT HAS GOT A BIT NIPPY."
POLICE BOX
WHY THE HELL WE BACK HERE? AIN'T NO DALEKS HERE!
IT'S... COMPLICATED.
COMPLICATED.
YOU REMEMBER ALL THAT WEIRD EQUIPMENT THE MASTER HAD?
THE TECHNOJUNK? HOLD IT -- STOP. CHANGED MY MIND. DON'T CARE DON'T CARE WHEN DO WE GET TO THE DAAAALEKS.
WELL, AMONGST THAT STUFF I NOTICED A... WELL...

"...A CHRONAL TUMOR."
THE FIRST TIME LORDS BELIEVED A CHRONAL TUMOR COULD BESTOW A KNACK FOR NAVIGATING THROUGH VORTEX OBSTACLES. INFECTED THEMSELVES ON PURPOSE.
DISGUSTING IDEA.
IT'D KILL US IF WE USED IT ON OURSELVES, BUT THE MASTER...? HE WIRED IT RIGHT INTO HIS TARDIS. H-HORRIBLE.
SMART.
ALSO I STILL DON'T CARE, IT'S STILL COMPLICATED, SKIP TO THE FRICKEN' END.
THE TUMOR'S INERT. BENIGN. I DON'T THINK THE MASTER EVER USED IT. SO IN ORDER TO ACTIVATE IT WE'D NEED, UH...
IT'S THEIR SHELLS, SEE? CARCINOGENIC AND ARTRONIC.
NEED WHAT?

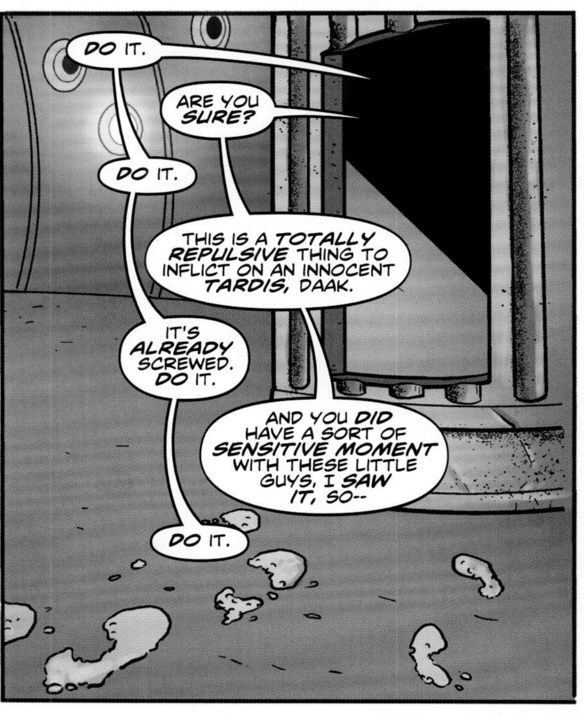
DO IT.
ARE YOU SURE?
DO IT.
THIS IS A TOTALLY REPULSIVE THING TO INFLICT ON AN INNOCENT TARDIS, DAAK.
IT'S ALREADY SCREWED. DO IT.
AND YOU DID HAVE A SORT OF SENSITIVE MOMENT WITH THESE LITTLE GUYS, I SAW IT, SO--
DO IT.

DAAK, IT'S... IT'S NOT NICE.
FINE. GIMME.
I'LL DO IT.

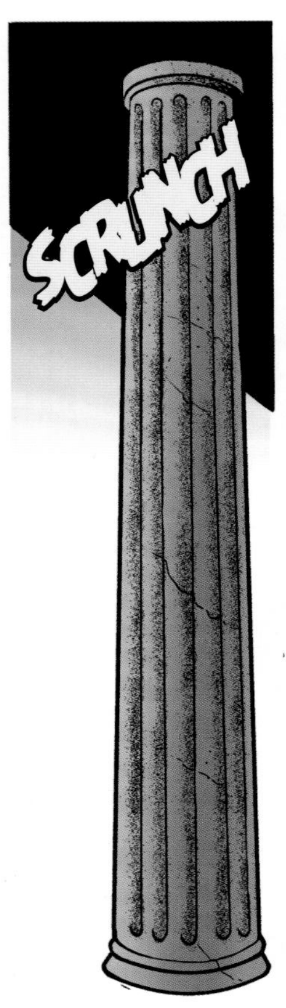
SCRUNCH

HUH. NEVER HEARD A TARDIS SCREAM BEFORE.
BLEUGH

W-WE NEED TO GET BACK TO SSHH. FROM THERE THE TIME WAR'S A STRAIGHT LINE BACKWARDS.
EH. BETTER HURRY. DON'T WANT THE SNOB INTERRUPTIN'.

...YOU, UM. YOU GET SOME REST.
I'LL BE RIGHT BACK.

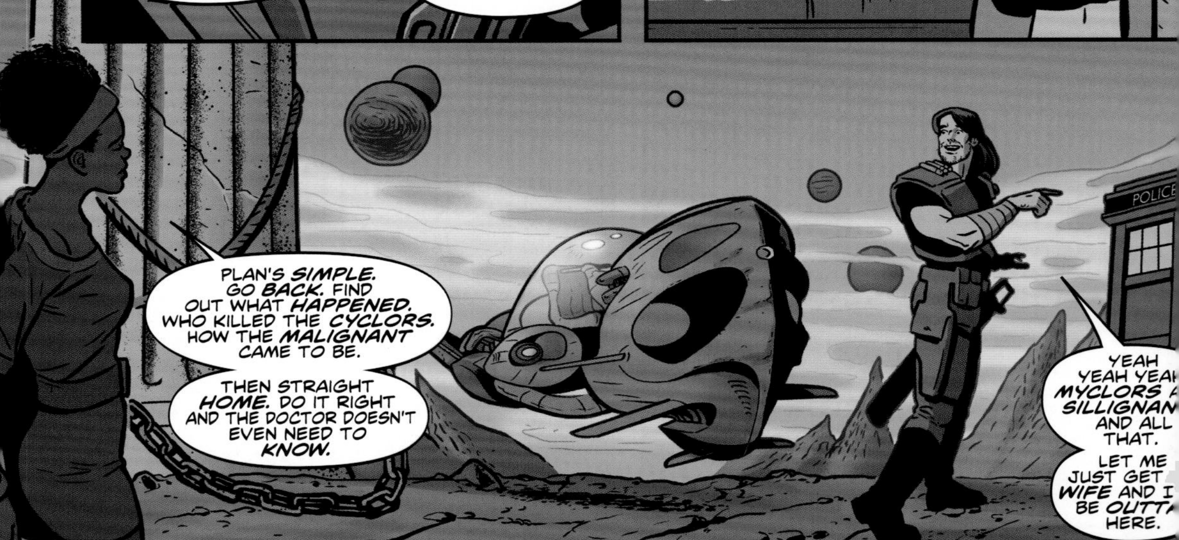
PLAN'S SIMPLE. GO BACK. FIND OUT WHAT HAPPENED. WHO KILLED THE CYCLORS. HOW THE MALIGNANT CAME TO BE.
THEN STRAIGHT HOME. DO IT RIGHT AND THE DOCTOR DOESN'T EVEN NEED TO KNOW.
POLICE
YEAH YEAH YEA MYCLORS A SILLIGNAN AND ALL THAT.
LET ME JUST GET WIFE AND I BE OUTTA HERE.

DAAK.
HUH?
I'M SORRY, DAAK.
?
THE BOUNTY HUNTER. I-IT'S CHASING ME. I'M THE LIABILITY.

I'M THE ONE WHO HASN'T EARNED HER SPOT."

IT HAS TO BE ME.
FUP

I'M SORRY.
WAIT.
NO, WAIT.
W...

NO NO NO NO NO
POLICE BOX

RIGHT THEN.

NO NO NO--
HH.
YES, ACTUALLY.
POLICE PUBLIC CALL BOX
POLICE PUBLIC CALL BOX
I'M AFRAID SO.

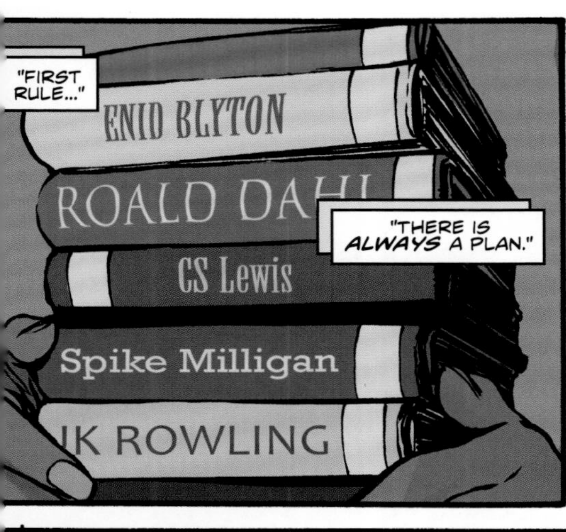
"FIRST RULE..."
ENID BLYTON
ROALD DAH
CS Lewis
Spike Milligan
K ROWLING
"THERE IS *ALWAYS* A PLAN."

SK.
WHAT KIND OF PHILISTINE ESN'T RESPECT LPHABETICAL ORDER?
JK ROWLING
JK ROWLING

COUGH
EXCUSE ME, MISS.
HMM?

YOU'RE ALICE OBIEFUNE, AREN'T YOU?
I... HOW DID YOU KNOW THAT?
I ASKED AT THE FRONT DESK AND THEY SAID YOU'D BEEN DEMOTED BECAUSE YOU WERE USELESS AND I COULD FIND YOU DOWN HERE.
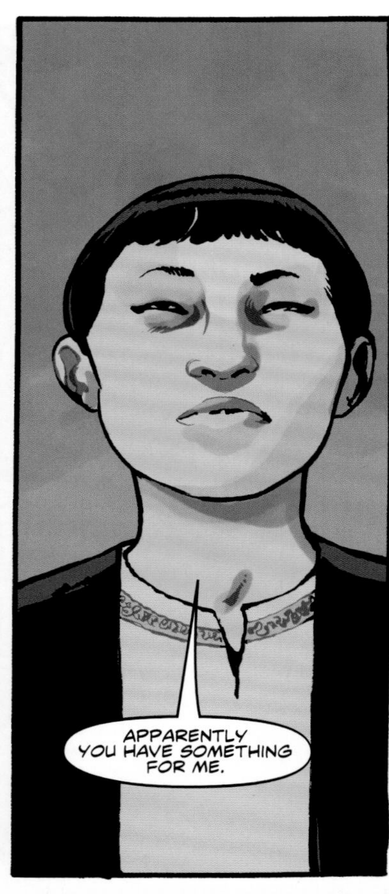
APPARENTLY YOU HAVE SOMETHING FOR ME.

WHAT?
SORRY, I'M NOT SURE WHAT YOU'RE...

OH HELL. WHAT... THAT'S... DISGUSTING.
SHLLLUUUUUURPPP

EWWW.
I'M GOING TO HAVE TO CLEAN THAT UP, AREN'T I?
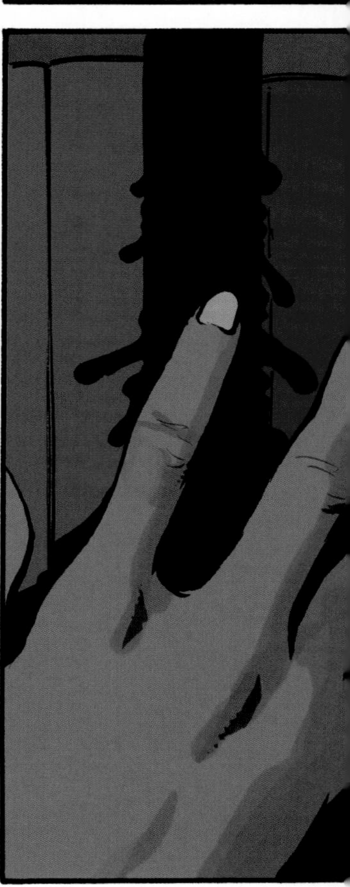

SHLLUUUUUPPP
AH...
SHLLUUUUUUUPPP
AH!
HU... HELP ME!
HELP ME!
SHLLUUUUUUUPPP
HE WAS RIGHT.
YOU ARE USELESS.
SHLLUUUUUUUPPP
NOOOOOOOOO!
"COME ON THEN."

FIRST RULE

MAN WITH A PLAN, RIGHT HERE!
EVIL MACHIAVELLIAN, MOUSTACHE-TWIRL-Y, WAR CRIME-LOVING, TOILET SEAT LEFT UP-ADORING DOCTOR, JUST WAITING FOR HIS COME-UPPANCE.
THE THEN AND THE NOW. THE MOST TERRIFYING, UNRELENTING BOUNTY HUNTER IN ALL THE UNIVERSE! NEVER FAILS TO BRING ITS PREY TO JUSTICE!
POLICE PUBLIC CALL BOX
NEVER ONCE FAILED!
WE STOP THE TARDIS FOR JUST SIXTY SECONDS AND YOU TURN UP. THERE IS NO ESCAPING YOU. YOU'RE DEATH AND TAXES. SO... COME ON, BIG BOY...
COME AND GET ME!

YOU CAN'T FIND ME, CAN YOU?
NOT ANY MORE.

SAVED... BY MY COMPANIONS. AS EVER.
...
COME ON, ALICE. COME BACK.

SQUIRE? YOU CONSCIOUS? HAS THE ROBO-MED DONE ITS MAGIC?

...HMMM. NOT QUITE YET.
DON'T WORRY, SQUIRE, ME OLD MYSTERY LADY. THE ROBO-MED'S A WONDER. YOU'LL BE UP AND ABOUT IN NO...

...TIME.

SO SMART, AIN'TCHA?
WITH ALL YER *PLANS.*

WHERE'S YOUR PLAN TO GET OUT OF THIS RIGHT HERE, EH? C'MON. ANSWER ME...
COME ON! ***WHERE'S YOUR PLAN?***

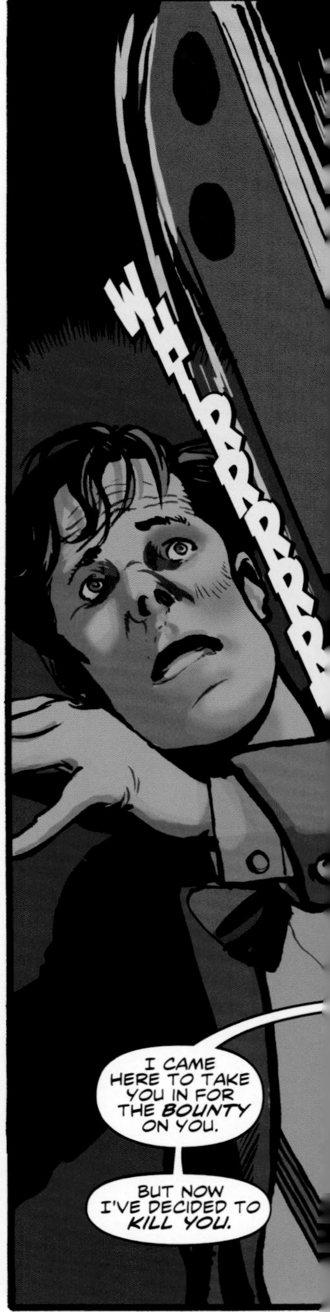
WHIRRRRR
I CAME HERE TO TAKE YOU IN FOR THE *BOUNTY* ON YOU.
BUT NOW I'VE DECIDED TO ***KILL YOU.***

SOMEWHERE IN THE TIME VORTEX.
THE MASTER'S TARDIS.
STOLEN BY ALICE OBIEFUNE.
YOU'D THINK THERE'D BE A MANUAL FOR FLYING THIS... BUT NO.
EVIL TIME LORDS WITH HORRIFIC CHRONAL TUMORS IN A JAR DON'T REALLY DO HELPFUL MANUALS, I SUPPOSE.
OKAY, STEAL THE MASTER'S TARDIS. GO BACK TO THE TIME WAR. WHICH IS IMPOSSIBLE. FIND THE VOLATIX CABAL, A SECRET DALEK SOCIETY THAT MAY NOT ACTUALLY EXIST.
FIND OUT WHO REALLY KILLED THE CYCLORS AND WHO CREATED THE MALIGNANT.
SAVE RIVER FROM HER MALIGNANT INFECTION.
DON'T DIE.
PRETTY STRAIGHT-FORWARD...

KRUNNNNCCHHHHH
AH!

THAT WAS THE BRAKES.
WE'VE STOPPED.
OH, YES. THAT WAS IT...

THERE WAS THAT BLOODY GREAT WALL STOPPING ANYONE TRAVELLING BACK TO THE TIME WAR.
TIME LOCKED.

IT'S... QUEASY IN HERE. SO DIFFICULT TO CONCENTRATE. LIKE YOU'RE DROWSY. IN AND OUT OF SLEEP. I THINK I HAD A NIGHTMARE ABOUT MY LIBRARY A WHILE AGO. LIKE A MIGRAINE IN MY...
... NECK ALL ALONG. IT WAS IN MY NECK AND HE KNEW. A CHRONO-TRACKER THAT ALLOWED THE THEN AND THE NOW TO FOLLOW US WHEREVER WE WENT.
I WAS PUTTING US ALL AT RISK.

... BETTER THAT I DO THIS ALONE.

COME ON! THE MASTER'S TARDIS WAS SUPPOSED TO BE ABLE TO GET ME IN!
HOW DO YOU GET INTO THE TIME WAR ANYWAY?

JUST CLICK YOUR HEELS TOGETHER THREE THOUSAND TIMES.
UNTIL THEY BLEED.
WHAT?

THERE WAS NO ACTUAL WAY A HUMAN COULD FLY INTO THE TIME WAR.
BUT YOU'VE ALREADY BEEN TO THE TIME WAR, HAVEN'T YOU?
YOU'RE NOT MOST HUMANS. TIME IS MALLEABLE, NOT LINEAR. YOU WERE THERE IN YOUR FUTURE, ALICE. DO YOU SEE?

HE DIDN'T WANT YOU, ALICE.
BUT I DO.
... NO.
HE HATES THEM ALL, ALICE. SECRETLY...
SLAM
BECAUSE THEY'RE ALWAYS STUPID ENOUGH TO FOLLOW HIM INTO HELL.

WHY DO YOU THINK HE RUNS?

I WILL TAKE YOU TO THE TIME WAR, ALICE OBIEFUNE.
"HEY! SPOT THE MASS MURDERER!"

IT'S *ME* ISN'T IT? I'M THE DUMB MONSTER, RIGHT! THE *BAD GUY!*
WELL, AT LEAST I DO MY OWN DIRTY WORK. I'M *HONEST* ABOUT THAT. BUT YOU?
I'M *NOTHING* COMPARED TO *YOU*. I'M AN *ANGEL*.

HANGE UR FACE THE TIME. HO DOES AT, EH?
THE UILTY. EOPLE ON RUN. ONLY RIMINALS O THAT.
RRRRRRRR

WHRRRRRRRRR
YOU *PLAY* WITH PEOPLE. PEOPLE WHO *TRUST* YOU. YOU MADE HER FEEL *WORTHLESS* AND THEN YOU SENT HER BACK...
... BACK TO THE WORST WAR IN...
THOKK
WHRRRRRRRRR
MORON!

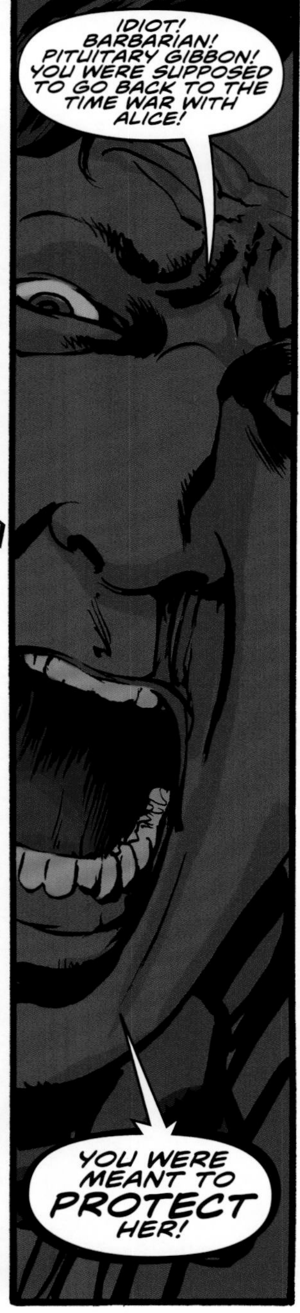
IDIOT! BARBARIAN! PITUITARY GIBBON! YOU WERE SUPPOSED TO GO BACK TO THE TIME WAR WITH ALICE!
YOU WERE MEANT TO PROTECT HER!

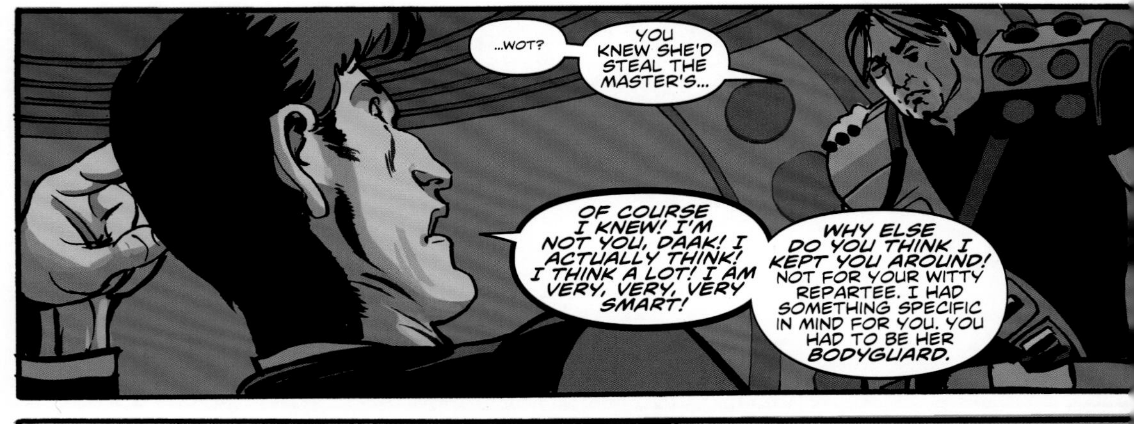
YOU KNEW SHE'D STEAL THE MASTER'S...
...WOT?
OF COURSE I KNEW! I'M NOT YOU, DAAK! I ACTUALLY THINK! I THINK A LOT! I AM VERY, VERY, VERY SMART!
WHY ELSE DO YOU THINK I KEPT YOU AROUND! NOT FOR YOUR WITTY REPARTEE. I HAD SOMETHING SPECIFIC IN MIND FOR YOU. YOU HAD TO BE HER BODYGUARD.

YOU WERE MEAN TO HER. SHE TOOK THE OTHER TARDIS.
I KNOW. I CAN'T GO BACK TO THE TIME WAR. THE TIMESTREAM WON'T ALLOW IT. BUT SHE COULD. SHE ALREADY HAS.
WHAT?
NOTHING...

I DIDN'T LIKE DOING IT, DAAK. I HATED IT. BUT WHAT CHOICE DID I HAVE?
RIVER'S GOING TO DIE. UNLESS WE FIND OUT WHAT THE MALIGNANT IS... WHAT CREATED IT. I CAN'T SAVE HER.
ALICE'S VISIONS. THEY WERE ALL OF HER BACK IN THE TIME WAR. SOME SORT OF TIME LOOP. SHE HAD TO GO BACK THERE.

AND SO I THOUGHT I'D SET IT UP SO YOU WOULD GO WITH HER. ALL THOSE LOVELY, LOVELY DALEKS FOR YOU TO KILL. HOW COULD YOU RESIST?
BUT IT TURNS OUT YOU WERE TOO MUCH OF A COWARD TO GO AND NOW SHE'S BACK THERE WITHOUT HER CHAINSWORD-WIELDING BODYGUARD.
... M'NOT STUPID.

SHE KNOCKED ME OUT. SAID SHE WAS THE ONE WHO HADN'T EARNED HER PLACE.
AND NOW SHE'S BACK THERE... ALONE.
OH DEAR...
YOU ARE SO BRAVE, ALICE OBIEFUNE.
LOOK AT YOU. LOOK HOW AMAZING YOU ARE.
YOU EARNED YOUR PLACE LONG AGO.
WOO OAWOOOOOOAWOOOOOOAHH!
WHAT'S THAT? IT'S THE THEN AND THE NOW, AIN'T IT?
NO. IT'S NOT...
EEEEEEEEEEEEEEEEEEEEEEEEEE!
OH NO...
DAAK! I NEED YOUR HELP!

WHUMP
"FIRST RULE.
"FIRST AND MOST IMPORTANT RULE OF BEING THE DOCTOR.

"THE COMPANIONS DO NOT DIE."
DAAK. HELP ME GET THE SQUIRE HOOKED UP TO THE MEDICAL APPARATUS! NOW!
THOUGHT YOU SAID THE ROBO-MED-THING WOULD HEAL HER.

IT SHOULD HAVE. HER WOUNDS WERE WITHIN ITS CAPABILITIES. EASILY. IT COULD HEAL A HUMAN WOUND OF THAT NATURE.

MAYBE SHE AIN'T HUMAN.
I CONSIDERED THAT! DO YOU HONESTLY THINK I DIDN'T CONSIDER THAT?

BUT ALL THE MED EQUIPMENT IS 100% CONVINCED SHE IS HUMAN. WITH A HUMAN HEART.
AND THAT HEART JU STOPPE

COME ON. COME ON. HURRY UP.
STUPID MACHINE! RESTART HER HEART!
"OH, RIVER. WHAT HAS HAPPENED TO ME?

"CAN'T SAVE YOU.
"CAN'T SAVE THE SQUIRE.
"AND I'VE SENT ALICE TO HER DEATH."

IT'S NOT WORKING, DOCTOR.

COME ON, SQUIRE. YOUR DOCTOR NEEDS YOU.
...PLEASE...

COME! ON!
RIIIIIIIIIIIIIP

AH!
COME ON!

START!
LIVE!

WHAT KIND OF DOCTOR AM I, EH?

WHAT KIND OF DOCTOR AM I?

"THE TROUBLE W
FIRST RULES...

"THEY'RE ALWAYS THE FIRST ONES TO BE BROKEN."
RAKKKKKLLLLLL... KRRRRRRRRKKKKKKKK...
RAKKKKKLLLLLL... KRRRRRRRRKKKKKKKK...
THOOOOOOOOOOOM
OMETHING...
COUGH
... I THINK SOMETHING TOOK CONTROL OF MY MIND.
I THINK THE TARDIS DID IT.
DID I MAKE IT.
IS THIS THE TIME WAR?

IT IS.

WHO ARE YOU, AND WHY DID YOU JUST TRY TO LAND THE MASTER'S *TARDIS* ON ME?

IT... IT'S YOU... ISN'T IT?
THE *TARDIS*, IT MUST HAVE BEEN TRYING TO FIND YOU.
YOU SOUND DIFFERENT... BUT YOUR EYES. I CAN *SEE YOU* IN THERE...

YOU'RE THE DOCTOR.
WHAT?
YOU ARE *WRONG*. THAT NAME IS DEAD AND BURIED. *NOW...*

TELL ME WHO SENT YOU OR I WILL BE FORCED TO COMPLETELY ATOMIZE YOU...
IN THE NAME OF *PEACE* AND *SANITY!*

RUUUU
MMBBBLLEEE
WHAT... WHAT'S HAPPENING?
AH!
THOOOOOOOOOOM
AHHHHHHHH!
THE TENDRILS!
VOLATIX TENDRILS!!
KATHOOOOOOM
DOCTOR!
I HAD A DREAM LIKE THIS! A NIGHTMARE! I THINK I DIE HERE!
HELP ME!!

DOCTOR!

DOCTOR! PLEASE!!!
I'M COMING!

I'M COMING!
COUGH

I'LL SAVE YOU.
"YES...
"THE FIRST RULE."

THE SQUIRE'S DEAD.

"THERE IS ALWAYS A PLAN."
TO BE CONTINUED!

COVER GALLERY

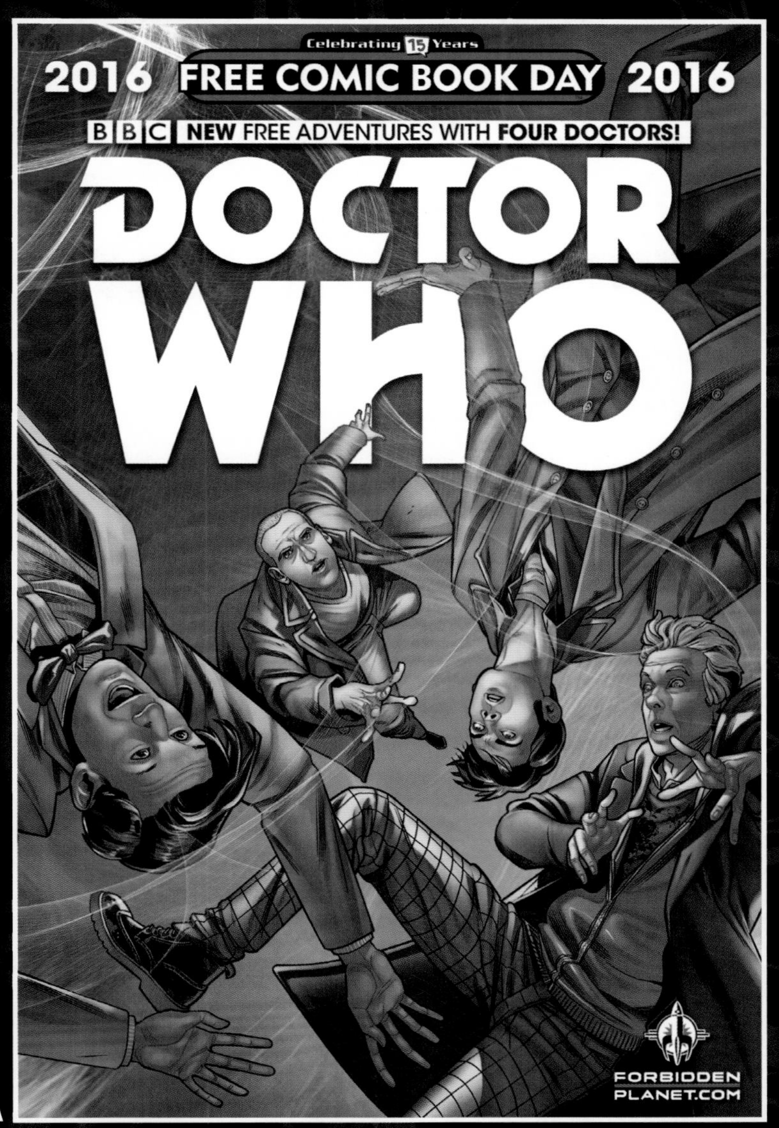

A

BBC THE ELEVENTH DOCTOR ADVENTURES YEAR TWO
DOCTOR WHO
ROB WILLIAMS
SIMON FRASER
GARY CALDWELL

B

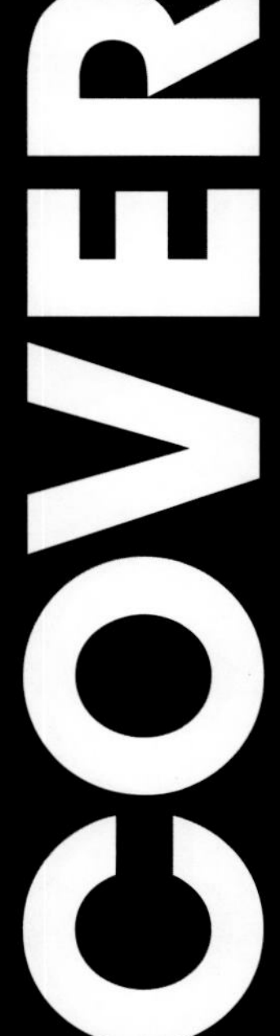

C

SSUES FCBD – #2.6

A: #FCBD Cover FP –
RACHAEL STOTT & IVAN NUNES
B: #2.6 Cover A – ALEX RONALD
C: #2.6 Cover C – QUESTION NO. 6

BBC DOCTOR WHO THE ELEVENTH DOCTOR

COVER GALLERY

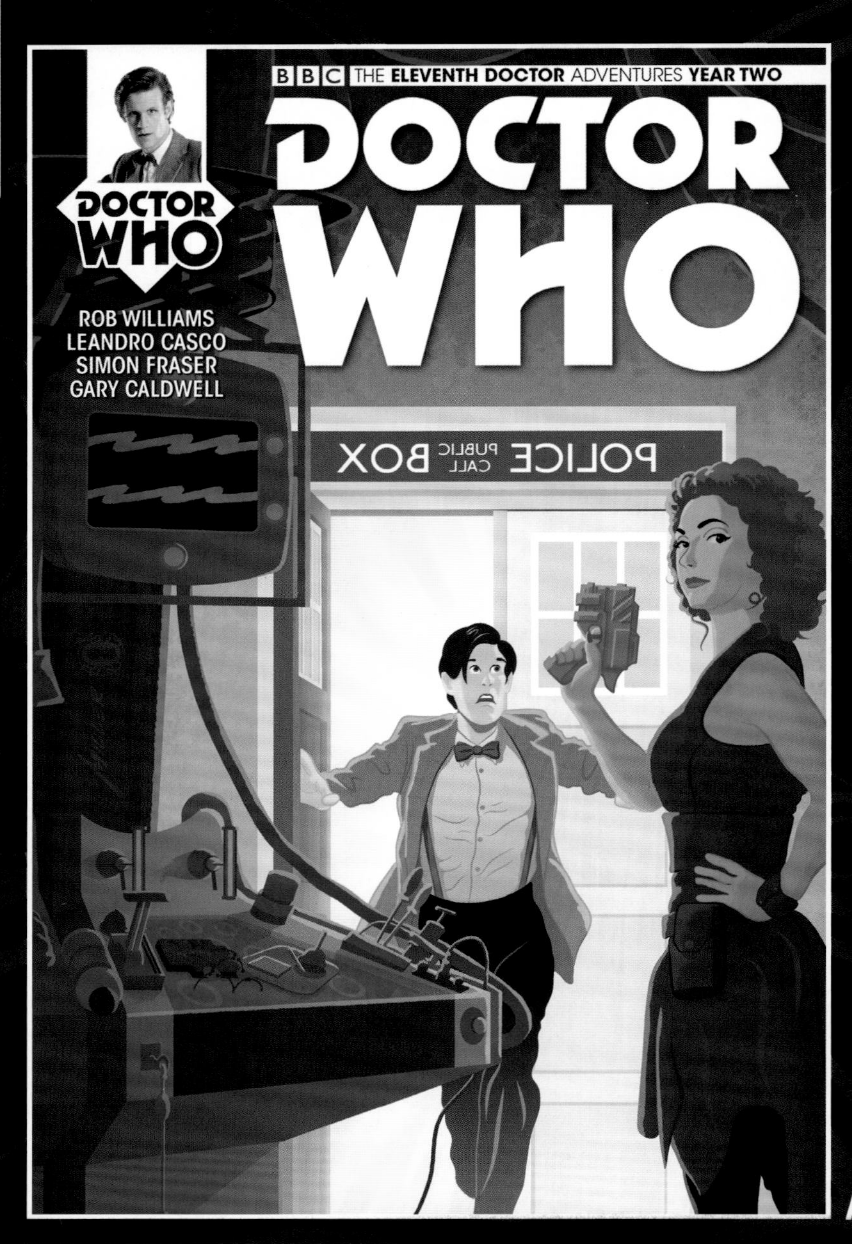

A

B

ISSUE #2.7

A: #2.7 Cover A – BRIAN MILLER & HI-FI
B: #2.7 Cover B – WILL BROOKS

COVER GALLERY

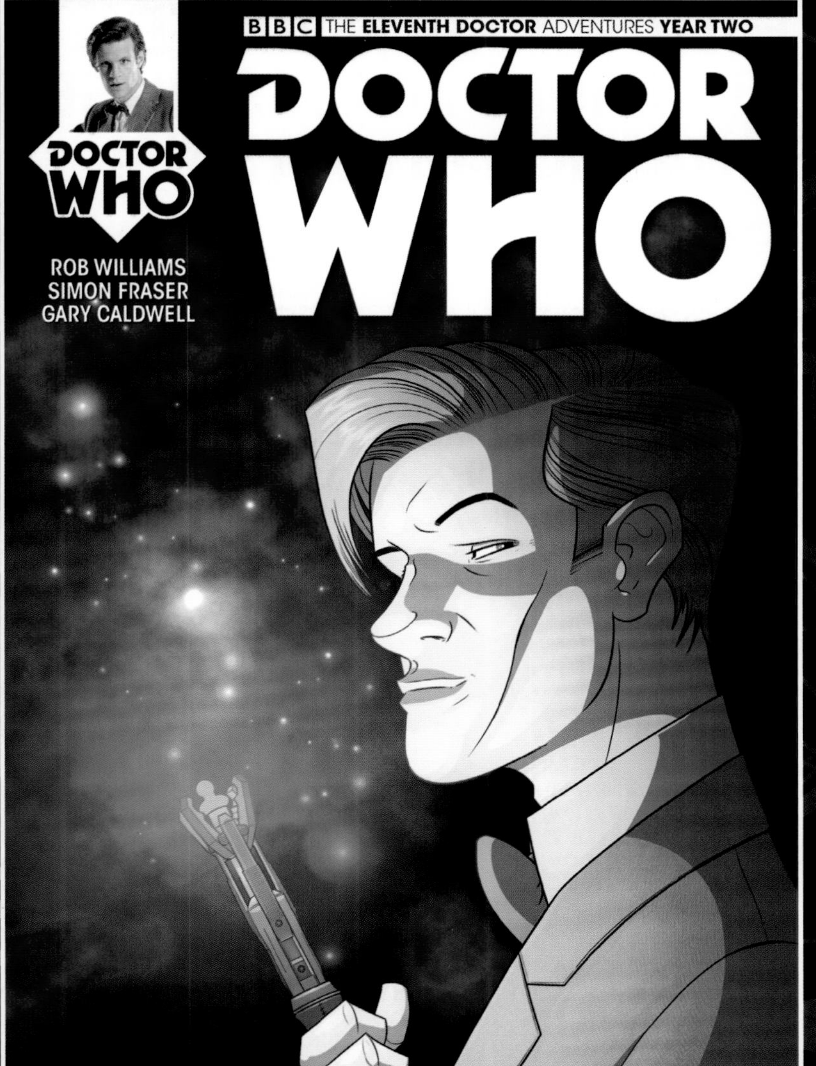

A

BBC THE ELEVENTH DOCTOR ADVENTURES YEAR TWO
DOCTOR WHO
DOCTOR WHO
POLICE TELEPHONE FREE FOR USE OF PUBLIC
PULL TO OPEN
ROB WILLIAMS
SIMON FRASER
GARY CALDWELL

B

ISSUE #2.10

A: #2.10 Cover A – DAN BOULTWOOD
B: #2.10 Cover C – ANDREW PEPOY & JASON MILLET

FOLLOW YOUR FAVORITE INCARNATIONS ACROSS THESE FANTASTIC COLLECTIONS!

DOCTOR WHO: THE TWELFTH DOCTOR VOL. 1: TERRORFORMER

ISBN: 9781782761778
ON SALE NOW - $19.99 / $22.95 CAN / £10.99
(UK EDITION ISBN: 9781782763864)

DOCTOR WHO: THE TWELFTH DOCTOR VOL. 2: FRACTURES

ISBN: 9781782763017
ON SALE NOW - $19.99 / $25.99 CAN / £10.99
(UK EDITION ISBN: 9781782766599)

DOCTOR WHO: THE TWELFTH DOCTOR VOL. 3: HYPERION

ISBN: 9781782767473
ON SALE NOW- $19.99 / $25.99 CAN / £10.99
(UK EDITION ISBN: 97817827674442)

DOCTOR WHO: THE TWELFTH DOCTOR VOL. 4: THE SCHOOL OF DEATH

ISBN: 9781785851087
COMING SOON - $19.99 / $25.99 CAN / £10.99
(UK EDITION ISBN: 9781785851070)

DOCTOR WHO: THE TENTH DOCTOR VOL. 1: REVOLUTIONS OF TERROR

ISBN: 9781782761747
ON SALE NOW - $19.99 / $22.95 CAN / £10.99
(UK EDITION ISBN: 9781782763840)

DOCTOR WHO: THE TENTH DOCTOR VOL. 2: THE WEEPING ANGELS OF MONS

ISBN: 9781782761754
ON SALE NOW - $19.99 / $25.99 CAN / £10.99
(UK EDITION ISBN: 9781782766575)

DOCTOR WHO: THE TENTH DOCTOR VOL. 3: THE FOUNTAINS OF FOREVER

ISBN: 9781782763024
ON SALE NOW - $19.99 / $25.99 CAN / £10.99
(UK EDITION ISBN: 9781782767435)

DOCTOR WHO: THE TENTH DOCTOR VOL. 4: THE ENDLESS SONG

ISBN: 9781785854286
ON SALE NOW - $19.99 / $25.99 CAN / £10.99
(SC ISBN: 9781785853227)

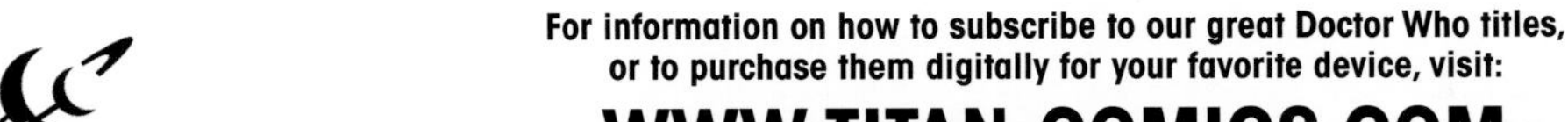

For information on how to subscribe to our great Doctor Who titles, or to purchase them digitally for your favorite device, visit:

WWW.TITAN-COMICS.COM

TITAN COMICS

COMPLETE YOUR COLLECTION!

)CTOR WHO:
IE ELEVENTH
)CTOR VOL. 1:
AFTER LIFE

: 9781782761747
LE NOW - $19.99 /
.95 CAN / £10.99
)N ISBN: 9781782763857)

DOCTOR WHO:
THE ELEVENTH
DOCTOR VOL. 2:
SERVE YOU

ISBN: 9781782761754
ON SALE NOW - $19.99 /
$25.99 CAN / £10.99
(UK EDITION ISBN: 9781782766582)

DOCTOR WHO:
THE ELEVENTH
DOCTOR VOL. 3:
CONVERSION

ISBN: 9781782763024
ON SALE NOW - $19.99 /
$25.99 CAN / £10.99
(UK EDITION ISBN: 9781782767435)

DOCTOR WHO:
THE ELEVENTH
DOCTOR VOL. 4:
THE THEN AND
THE NOW

ISBN: 9781782767466
ON SALE NOW - $19.99 /
$25.99 CAN / £10.99
(UK EDITION ISBN: 9781722767428)

DOCTOR WHO: THE NINTH DOCTOR
VOL. 1: WEAPONS OF PAST DESTRUCTION

ISBN: 9781782763369
ON SALE NOW - $19.99 / $25.99 CAN / £10.99
(UK EDITION ISBN: 9781782761056)

DOCTOR WHO EVENT 2015
FOUR DOCTORS

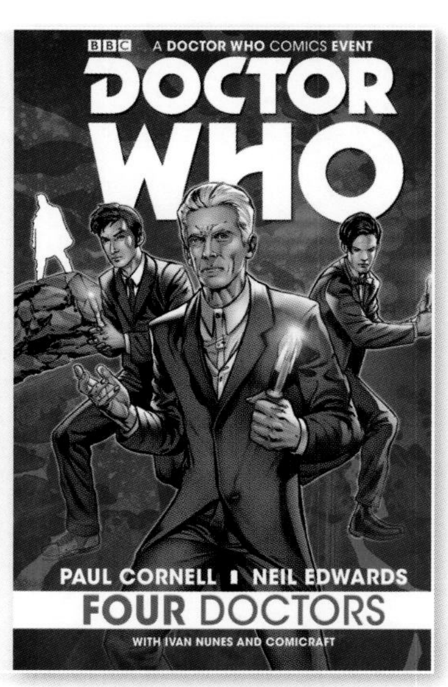

ISBN: 9781782765967
ON SALE NOW - $19.99 / $25.99 CAN / £10.99
(UK EDITION ISBN: 9781785851063)

AVAILABLE IN ALL GOOD COMIC STORES, BOOK STORES, AND DIGITAL PROVIDERS!

BIOGRAPHIES

Si Spurrier has written often for *2000 AD* and *Judge Dredd Magazine*, and continues to produce ambitious work in both prose and comics. He is best known for writing titles such as *X-Force* and *X-Men: Legacy* for Marvel, and his creator-owned titles *The Spire* and *Six-Gun Gorilla* at BOOM!, *Cry Havoc* at Image, and *Numbercruncher* at Titan Comics.

Rob Williams began his comics career with *CLA$$WAR*, and now writes stunning work for *2000AD (Judge Dredd: Titan, Low Life, Trifecta, Ichabod Azrael)* DC (*Suicide Squad, Martian Manhunter*), Vertigo (*Unfollow, The Royals*), and Titan, which also publishes his creator-owned *Ordinary.* He lives in Bristol, UK.

Simon Fraser is a world-traveling artist, born in Scotland, now based in New York City. Best known as the co-creator of *Nikolai Dante for 2000AD*, Fraser has drawn for *Judge Dredd, Grindhouse, Family, Hell House* and his own series, *Lilly MacKenzie*.

Warren Pleece is a comic artist and graphic novelist of over 20 years experience – working for *2000AD*, DC, Dark Horse and many more – on titles such as *True Faith, Hellblazer, The Invisibles, Deadenders* and *Incognegro*. He lives in Brighton, UK.

Gary Caldwell has been coloring Simon Fraser's work for over twenty years, as Simon's right-hand man. Based in Scotland, he quietly knocks his pages out of the park every time.

Hi-Fi Colour Design was founded in 1998 by Brian and Kristy Miller and provides digital color for comic books, toys, video games, and animation, and tutorials on color through masterdigitalcolor.com.

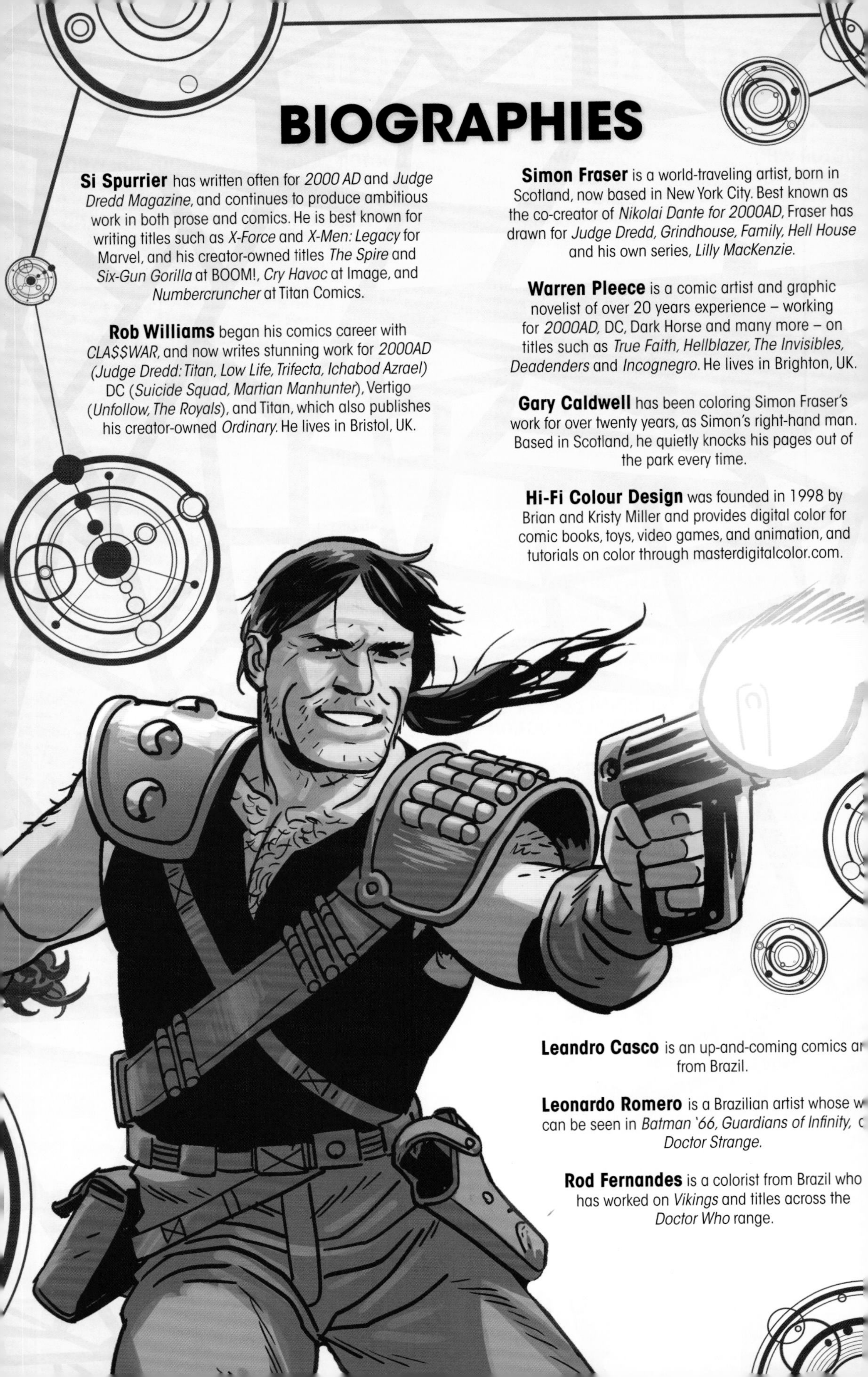

Leandro Casco is an up-and-coming comics ar
from Brazil.

Leonardo Romero is a Brazilian artist whose w
can be seen in *Batman '66, Guardians of Infinity,* c
Doctor Strange.

Rod Fernandes is a colorist from Brazil who has worked on *Vikings* and titles across the *Doctor Who* range.